**STRATEGIES**
for Writers

# Practice the Strategy

## Notebook

### Level D

## Authors

**Leslie W. Crawford, Ed.D.**
Georgia College & State University

**Rebecca Bowers Sipe, Ed.D.**
Eastern Michigan University

**Cover Design**
Tommaso Design Group

**Art Credits**
p30, Ralph Canaday; pp74, 122, Linda Bittner

**Production by** Inkwell Publishing Solutions, Inc.

**ISBN 0-7367-1246-1**

Zaner-Bloser, Inc., P.O. Box 16764, Columbus, Ohio 43216-6764   (1-800-421-3018)

Printed in the United States of America

03   04   05   06   MZ   5   4   3

# Table of Contents

## NARRATIVE
### writing

## DESCRIPTIVE
### writing

# EXPOSITORY
## writing

# NARRATIVE
## writing

## PERSUASIVE

### writing

## TEST

### writing

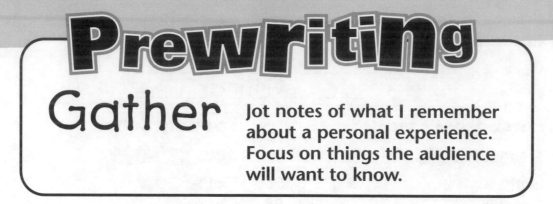

**Gather** Jot notes of what I remember about a personal experience. Focus on things the audience will want to know.

**Now it's your turn to practice this strategy with different topics.**
Read these notes about the day one writer's family got its first computer.

### What I Remember

- Everyone in the neighborhood already had one!

- All the kids in school were already on-line.

- It was bright blue.

- I begged my parents to get a computer.

- We had arguments about who was going on-line first.

- Mom and Dad acted as if it was a big deal. (It was!)

- It took hours to set up! Everybody was getting tense!

- Dad looked for just the right computer.

- Mom looked for the best price.

- They had to read everything and talk to everyone.

# Prewriting

## Gather

Jot notes of what I remember about a personal experience. Focus on things the audience will want to know.

**your own writing**

What do you remember about a day when your family got something important or exciting? Jot down what you recall. If you need to make up some details, you may do so.

### What I Remember

_____

_____

_____

_____

_____

_____

_____

_____

_____

_____

_____

_____

**RETURN** Now go back to Davina's work on page 19 in the Student Edition.

# PreWriting
## Organize
Use my notes to make a sequence chain.

**Now it's time for you to practice this strategy.** Read the notes below. The writer selected the notes on page 6 that named events and organized them in the sequence chain below.

| The Day We Got Our New Computer | |
| --- | --- |
| **First Event** | All the kids in school were already on-line. |
| **Second Event** | I begged my parents to get a computer. |
| **Third Event** | Dad looked for the right computer. |
| **Fourth Event** | Mom looked for the best price. |
| **Fifth Event** | It took hours to set up. |
| **Last Event** | We had arguments about who was going on-line first. |

# Prewriting

## Organize   Use my notes to make a sequence chain.

**your own writing**

**Now it's time for you to practice this strategy.** Use the notes you took on page 7. Select the notes that name events and organize them in the sequence chain below. Add events if you need to.

| |
|---|

**First Event**

**Second Event**

**Third Event**

**Fourth Event**

**Fifth Event**

**Last Event**

**RETURN** Now go back to Davina's work on page 20 in the Student Edition.

**Narrative Writing** • Personal Narrative

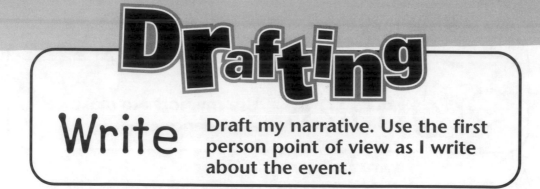

# Write

**Draft my narrative. Use the first person point of view as I write about the event.**

Writing in the first person means using the pronouns *I, we, me, my,* and *mine* to show the readers that you are part of the story. Read the draft of the day the writer's family got its first computer. (You will see some mistakes. You will have a chance to correct them on later pages.) Circle the words that show writing in the first person.

For a while, we seemed to be the only family in town

without a computer. All my friends went home and they did

homework and they played computer games and they sent

e-mail. I went home and begged Mom and Dad to get us a

computer.

My parents talked about it forever. My dad had

to get just the right computer. Mom wanted to get the very

best price.

# Drafting

## Write

Draft my narrative. Use the first person point of view as I write about the event.

**your own writing**

Use the lines below to write a draft of the day your family got something important or exciting. Use the sequence chain you filled in on page 9 to write your draft. Remember to use the first person point of view as you write.

_____

_____

_____

_____

_____

_____

_____

_____

_____

_____

_____

_____

**RETURN** Now go back to Davina's work on page 22 in the Student Edition.

**Revising**

# Elaborate

Look for places to add clear and interesting details.

your own writing

**Now it's time for you to practice this strategy.** Read this draft of a personal narrative about the day that one writer's family got its first computer. (You will see some errors. You can fix them now or leave them until later.) As you read the draft, ask yourself each question in the margin. Use your answer to write a specific detail on the line.

For a while, we seemed to be the only family in

**What did they do on their computers?**

town without a computer. All my friends went

home from school and got on their computers.

_____

_____

**What did Dad do to get the right computer?**

They talked about it forever. Dad had to get just

the right computer.

_____

_____

**What did they do to get what they wanted?**

Mom wanted to get the very best price. Dad

wanted specific features. A mess!

_____

_____

# Revising

# Elaborate
Look for places to add clear and interesting details.

**How did I feel about that?**

Finally, the day came when Mom and Dad agreed.

We went to the store, where Mom and Dad asked

more questions.

_____

_____

_____

**What did I see?**

Finally, we heard the sound the computer makes

when it's working. At last, ready to go!

_____

_____

_____

**How did I feel about that?**

Then, of course, came the arguments about who

was going on-line first.

_____

_____

_____

_____

**RETURN** Now go back to Davina's paper on page 23 in the Student Edition.

# ReVising
## Clarify
Look for stringy sentences and separate them.

**Now it's time for you to practice this strategy.** Read each stringy sentence below. Rewrite it by separating it into two or more sentences.

**1.** All my classmates went home and they did their homework and they played computer games and they sent e-mail.

_____

_____

_____

**2.** Dad had to get just the right computer and he spent lots of time reading and shopping and he seemed to be planning a trip to Mars!

_____

_____

_____

**3.** Then, of course, came the arguments about who was going on-line first but these still happen quite a bit but I suppose this will always be a problem.

_____

_____

_____

**4.** Still, we've got a computer now so I tell everyone I know about it and I think they are tired of hearing about it.

_____

_____

Remember:
Use this strategy in
your own
writing

_____

RETURN
Now go back to Davina's paper on page 24 in the Student Edition.

**Narrative Writing** • Personal Narrative

# Proofread

Check to see that there are no sentence fragments.

| | |
|---|---|
| ⊐ Indent. | ℓ Take out something. |
| ≡ Make a capital | ⊙ Add a period. |
| / Make a small letter | ⌗ New paragraph |
| ∧ Add something. | SP Spelling error |

**Now it's time for you to practice this strategy.** Here is the revised draft of the personal narrative about the day one writer's family finally got a computer. Use the proofreading marks to correct any errors. Use a dictionary to help with spelling.

For a while, we seemed to be the only family in town without a computer. All my friends went home from school and got on the computers. They did their homework. They played computer games. They sent e-mail. I begged Mom and Dad to get us a computer.

They talked about it forever. Had to get just the right computer. Lots of time reading and shopping! He seemed to be planning a trip to Mars! Mom wanted to get the very best price. Dad wanted specific fectures. A mess! Finally, we went to the store and picked out are new computer.

It took Hours and hours to set up the new computer. Finally, we heard the sound a computer makes when it's working. The screen showed the icons for all our programs. At last, ready to go!

Then, of course, came the arguments about who was going on-line first. Still, weve got a computer now and I tell everyone I know about it.

**Remember:** Use this strategy in *your own writing*

RETURN Now go back to Davina's paper on page 26 in the Student Edition.

**Narrative Writing** • Personal Narrative  15

# Using a

**Rubric**

Use this rubric to assess Davina's personal narrative on page 27 in your Student Edition. You may work with a partner.

**Audience**

How well does the writer focus on things the audience will want to know?

**Organization**

Do events follow each other in order?

**Elaboration**

How well does the writer use clear and interesting details to describe people and events?

**Clarification**

Does the writer avoid stringing sentences together with *and, and, and* or ?

**your own writing**

Save this rubric. Use it to check your own writing.

**Conventions & SKILLS**

Are there any sentence fragments?

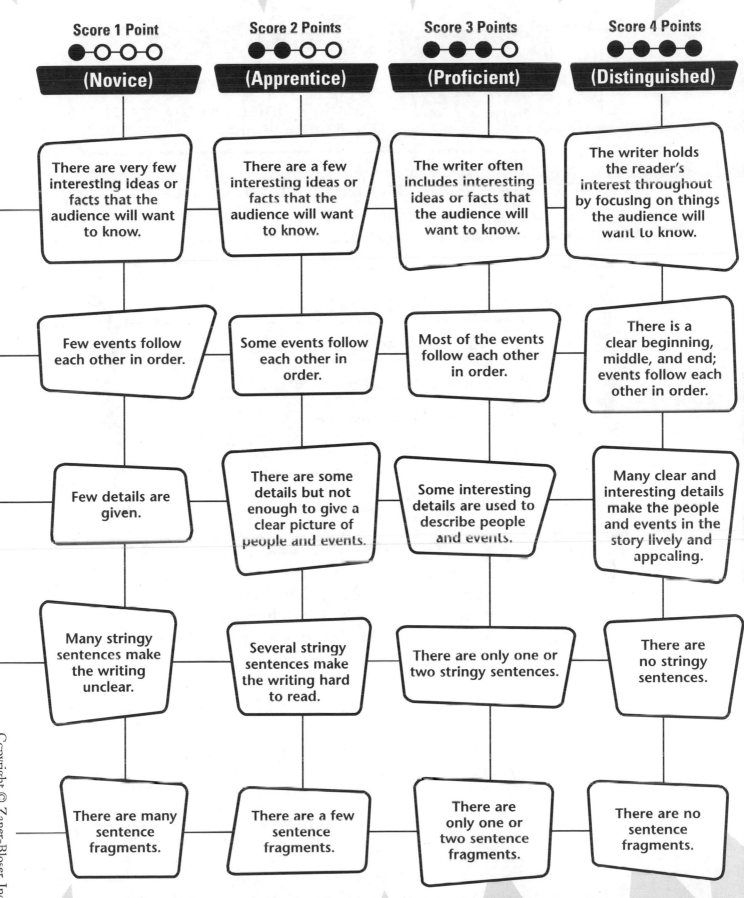

**Score 1 Point**
● ○ ○ ○
**(Novice)**

**Score 2 Points**
● ● ○ ○
**(Apprentice)**

**Score 3 Points**
● ● ● ○
**(Proficient)**

**Score 4 Points**
● ● ● ●
**(Distinguished)**

There are very few interesting ideas or facts that the audience will want to know.

There are a few interesting ideas or facts that the audience will want to know.

The writer often includes interesting ideas or facts that the audience will want to know.

The writer holds the reader's interest throughout by focusing on things the audience will want to know.

Few events follow each other in order.

Some events follow each other in order.

Most of the events follow each other in order.

There is a clear beginning, middle, and end; events follow each other in order.

Few details are given.

There are some details but not enough to give a clear picture of people and events.

Some interesting details are used to describe people and events.

Many clear and interesting details make the people and events in the story lively and appealing.

Many stringy sentences make the writing unclear.

Several stringy sentences make the writing hard to read.

There are only one or two stringy sentences.

There are no stringy sentences.

There are many sentence fragments.

There are a few sentence fragments.

There are only one or two sentence fragments.

There are no sentence fragments.

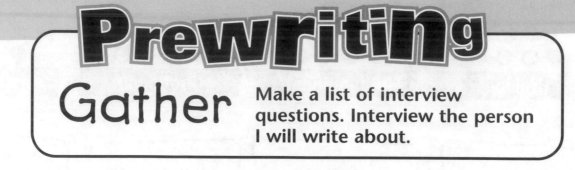

# Prewriting

## Gather

Make a list of interview questions. Interview the person I will write about.

**Now it's your turn to practice this strategy with different topics.** Read these questions. A writer wrote them before interviewing Mrs. Roos, who had laser eye surgery.

- What eye problems did you have?

- Why did you decide to have laser surgery?

- What happened during the surgery?

- How did you feel after the surgery?

- Did you face any risks?

- Are you glad you did it?

Now think of some questions you would like to ask an interesting person you know. Interview the person and write down his or her answers to your questions. Write your questions on the lines below.

_____

_____

_____

_____

_____

 Now go back to Ashley's work on page 37 in the Student Edition.

# Prewriting

## Organize
Use what I've learned to make a time line.

Here are the answers Mrs. Roos gave when she was interviewed about her eye surgery. As you read the answers, think about how you could put them in order on a time line.

- I was always very nearsighted. I got my first glasses in 1970 when I was six. In 1985, I got contact lenses. By 1995, I couldn't wear the lenses anymore because they weren't right for my eyes.

- I couldn't see as well with glasses as I had with contact lenses. The situation got worse and worse. In 1999, I met with an eye surgeon. She told me what could be done. I decided to take a chance.

- One year later, I had surgery. The whole thing took about fifteen minutes. My eyes were numb, so I didn't feel anything except one tiny pinch.

- After the surgery, I could see perfectly. I had to wear big plastic lenses over my eyes for one day and three nights. That was mainly to keep me from rubbing my eyes.

- One risk of this surgery is that the cut can be the wrong size. Then you won't get the results you want, or you'll get a new problem.

- It's now a year later, and I'm glad I had the surgery. I can see perfectly the minute I wake up in the morning. I participate in sports with confidence.

Now turn to page 20 of this book. Use the time line on page 20 to organize these notes.

# Prewriting

## Organize

Use what I've learned to make a time line.

**Now it's time for you to practice this strategy.** Use the time line below to organize the notes on Mrs. Roos's laser eye surgery. The dates are provided for you.

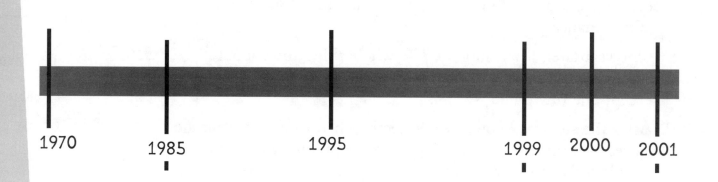

1970    1985    1995    1999    2000    2001

**Narrative Writing** • Biographic Sketch

# Prewriting

## Organize  Use what I've learned to make a time line.

your own writing

**Now it's time for you to practice this strategy.** Use the answers you wrote down during your own interview to fill in the time line below.

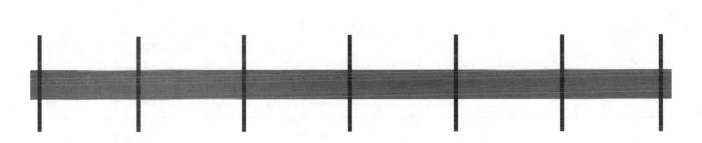

 Now go back to Ashley's work on page 38 in the Student Edition.

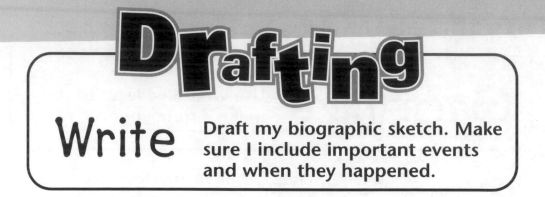

# Write

**Draft my biographic sketch. Make sure I include important events and when they happened.**

**Now it's time for you to practice this strategy.** Look back at the time line you filled in on page 20. Now write about the events in order.

_____

_____

_____

_____

_____

_____

_____

_____

_____

_____

_____

**Remember:** Use this strategy in **your own writing**

## Write

Draft my biographic sketch. Make sure I include important events and when they happened.

your own writing

**Now it's time for you to practice this strategy.** Look at the time line you created on page 21 of this book. Use the lines below, your interview questions, and your time line to write a draft of your own biographic sketch. Remember to include important events and when they happened.

_____

_____

_____

_____

_____

_____

_____

_____

_____

_____

Now go back to Ashley's work on page 40 in the Student Edition.

# Revising

## Elaborate  Add more interesting information about the person.

**Now it's time for you to practice this strategy**. The bulleted items in the box below are interesting details about Mrs. Roos. Decide where they fit in this essay. Rewrite them as complete sentences and add them. You will see some errors. You will have a chance to correct them on the next few pages.

---

- can see perfectly the minute I wake up in the morning
- had to wear big plastic lenses over my eyes for one day and three nights
- eyes were numb; didn't feel anything except one tiny pinch

---

_____

In 2000, Mrs. Roos took the risk. The surgury were easy! _____

_____

The surgin used the laser. Fifteen minutes later, it were over.

_____

Everything else was perfect. _____

**Remember:** Use this strategy in **your own writing**

Now go back to Ashley's work on page 41 in the Student Edition.

# ReVising

## Clarify

Look for places to add time-order signal words to show how events follow one another.

**Now it's time for you to practice this strategy.** Read this draft of the biographic sketch about Mrs. Roos. The words in the box are time-order signal words and phrases. Decide where they fit in this draft. Add them.

| finally | then | soon | at first |
|---|---|---|---|

In 1970, Mrs. Roos was just six years old. She was so

nearsighted that she needs unusully strong glasses. In 1985

she tried contact linses. Her vision improved alot, but she

coud not were those either.

Many years passed. Mrs. Roos's eyesight were a problem.

She could not see much intil she put on her glasses.

In 1999, Mrs. Roos met with an eye surgin. She told Mrs.

Roos about a new laser surgury that could fix her eyesight.

Remember: Use this strategy in your own writing

Now go back to Ashley's work on page 42 in the Student Edition.

*Narrative Writing* • Biographic Sketch

| | | |
|---|---|---|
| ⌐ Indent. | ℓ Take out something. |
| ≡ Make a capital. | ⊙ Add a period. |
| / Make a small letter. | �# New paragraph |
| ∧ Add something. | SP Spelling error |

# Editing

## Proofread
Check to see that all subjects and verbs agree.

**Now it's time for you to practice this strategy.** Here is the revised draft of the biographic sketch about Mrs. Roos's laser eye surgery. Use the proofreading marks to correct the errors.

In 1970, Mrs. Roos was just six years old. She was so

nearsighted that she needs unusully strong glasses. Then, in

1985, she tried contact linses. At first, her vision improved

alot, but soon she coud not were those either.

Many years passed. Mrs. Roos's eyesight were a problem.

She could not see much intil she put on her glasses.

Finally, in 1999, Mrs. Roos met with an eye surgin. She told

Mrs. Roos about a new laser surgury that could fix her

eyesight. She found out that she could be helped. She also

learned about some risks. Sometimes, laser surgury create

new problems most of the time it turn out fine.

**Remember:**
Use this strategy in
*your own writing*

# Editing

## Proofread

Check that subjects and verbs agree.

In 2000, Mrs. Roos took the risk. The surgury were easy!

First, her eyes were numbed, so she didn't feel anything

except one tiny pinch. The surgin used the laser. Fifteen

minutes later, it were over. She had to wear big plastic

lenses to protect her eyes for one day and three nights.

Everything else was perfect. Now she can see perfectly the

minute she wakes up in the morning.

Mrs. Roos look back at her surgury with pride. She see

without glasses or contact lenses now. She even participates

in sports with confidence. She is very glad that she took

the risk and had the surgury done.

**Remember:** Use this strategy in **your own writing**

RETURN Now go back to Ashley's work on page 44 in the Student Edition.

# Using a  Rubric

Use this rubric to evaluate Ashley's biographic sketch on page 45 in your Student Edition. You may work with a partner.

 **Audience**

How well does the writer create interest for the audience?

 **Organization**

Does the writer include important events and when they happened?

**Elaboration**

Does the writer include interesting information about the person?

**Clarification**

Does the writer use time-order signal words to show how events follow one another?

 **your own writing**

Save this rubric. Use it to check your own writing.

 **Conventions & Skills**

Do subjects and verbs agree?

| Score 1 Point | Score 2 Points | Score 3 Points | Score 4 Points |
|---|---|---|---|
| ●○○○ | ●●○○ | ●●●○ | ●●●● |
| **(Novice)** | **(Apprentice)** | **(Proficient)** | **(Distinguished)** |

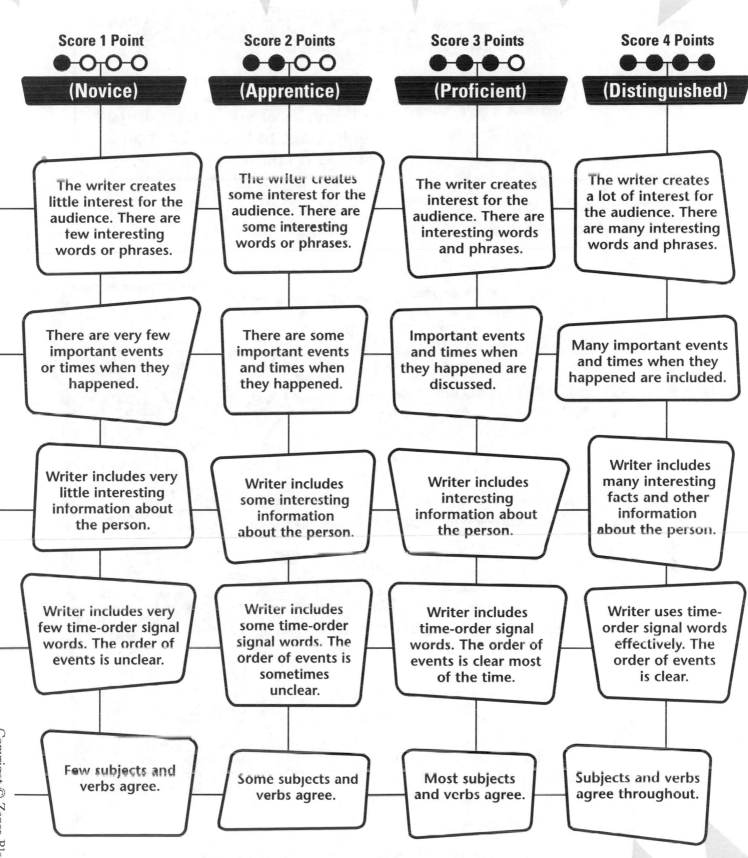

The writer creates little interest for the audience. There are few interesting words or phrases.

The writer creates some interest for the audience. There are some interesting words or phrases.

The writer creates interest for the audience. There are interesting words and phrases.

The writer creates a lot of interest for the audience. There are many interesting words and phrases.

There are very few important events or times when they happened.

There are some important events and times when they happened.

Important events and times when they happened are discussed.

Many important events and times when they happened are included.

Writer includes very little interesting information about the person.

Writer includes some interesting information about the person.

Writer includes interesting information about the person.

Writer includes many interesting facts and other information about the person.

Writer includes very few time-order signal words. The order of events is unclear.

Writer includes some time-order signal words. The order of events is sometimes unclear.

Writer includes time-order signal words. The order of events is clear most of the time.

Writer uses time-order signal words effectively. The order of events is clear.

Few subjects and verbs agree.

Some subjects and verbs agree.

Most subjects and verbs agree.

Subjects and verbs agree throughout.

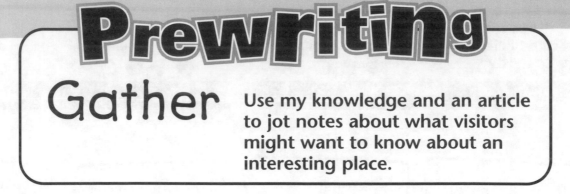

# Prewriting

## Gather
Use my knowledge and an article to jot notes about what visitors might want to know about an interesting place.

Read this article about an old, mysterious house in the small town of Pleasant Valley.

One of the most interesting spots to visit in Pleasant Valley is the Shroud Estate. Clyde Shroud built it in 1884 for his new bride. Nobody ever saw the mysterious Charlotte Shroud. The Shrouds lived in their new home for only a few years. In 1901, the entire family disappeared from Pleasant Valley. Nobody knows where they went.

The Shroud Estate sits on top of the highest bluff like a guard overlooking Pleasant Valley. The heavy oak door is locked. The windows are boarded up. The tall trees enclose the house in a blanket of gloom.

A rusted iron fence surrounds the mansion. Many visitors have come to the Shroud Estate. They hope to solve the hundred-year-old mystery. Who will unlock the secrets this house holds? Maybe it will be you.

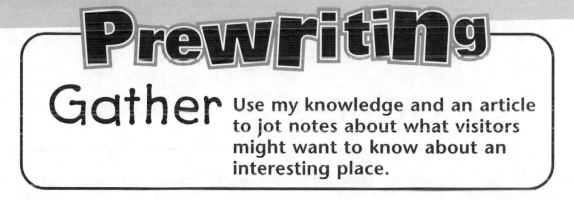

# Gather

Use my knowledge and an article to jot notes about what visitors might want to know about an interesting place.

**Now it's your turn to practice this strategy with a different topic.** Have you ever seen a mysterious old house? Use your own knowledge and the article and picture on the opposite page to jot some notes about what you might hear, see, touch, taste, and smell.

### Notes on a Mysterious House

_____

_____

_____

_____

_____

_____

_____

_____

_____

_____

**RETURN** Now go back to Sandra's work on page 57 in the Student Edition.

**Descriptive Writing** · Descriptive Paragraph

# Prewriting

## Organize   Use my notes to make a web.

your own writing

**Now it's time for you to practice this strategy.** Use your notes on page 31 (about the mysterious house) to make a web. Write the main topic in the center circle. Write the details in the other circles.

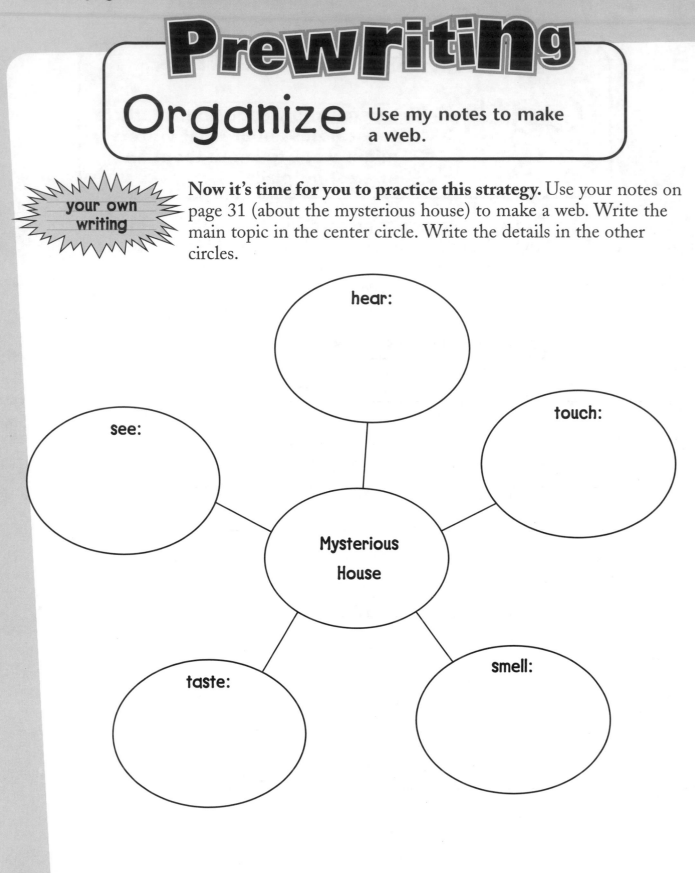

hear:

touch:

see:

Mysterious House

taste:

smell:

RETURN Now go back to Sandra's work on page 58 in the Student Edition.

**Descriptive Writing** • Descriptive Paragraph

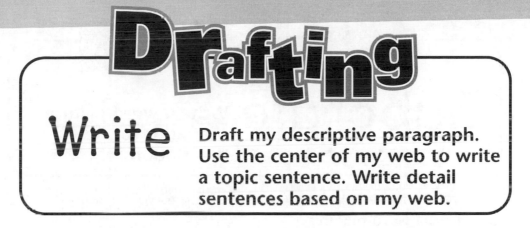

**Write** Draft my descriptive paragraph. Use the center of my web to write a topic sentence. Write detail sentences based on my web.

**Now it's time for you to practice this strategy.** Look at the center of the web you filled in on page 32. The main topic is *mysterious house*. Which sentence below would make the best topic sentence for a descriptive paragraph? Circle it.

**1.** I know a mysterious house.

**2.** Just looking at the mysterious old house on the hill outside of town can give you a chill.

**3.** The old house on the edge of town has boarded-up windows.

Now use what you wrote in the other circles in the web to write detail sentences.

**Detail Sentence:**

_____

_____

**Detail Sentence:**

_____

_____

**Detail Sentence:**

_____

_____

Now go back to Sandra's work on page 60 in the Student Edition.

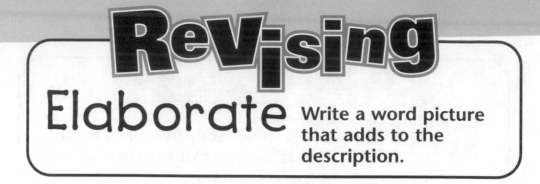

**Revising**

# Elaborate

**Write a word picture that adds to the description.**

What information would be more interesting to your reader if you added a word picture?

**Now it's time for you to practice this strategy.** Look on page 33 and read the detail sentences you wrote about a mysterious old house. Choose one sentence that would be more interesting if you added a word picture. Word pictures are descriptions that use words and phrases that help the reader "see" what the writer is describing. Read the example below.

**Detail sentence:** The big evergreen trees make the house look dark.

**Word picture:** They surround it like ancient guards, wrapping it in a shadow of mystery.

**your own writing** Use the lines below to write a word picture for one of the detail sentences you wrote on page 33.

**Detail Sentence**

_____

_____

**Word Picture**

_____

_____

 Now go back to Sandra's work on page 61 in the Student Edition.

Use after page 61 in the Student Edition.

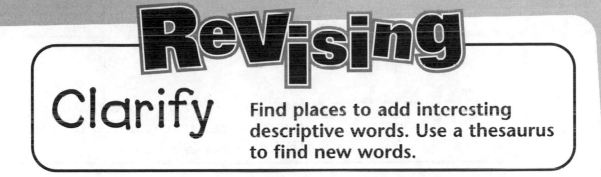

# Clarify

Find places to add interesting descriptive words. Use a thesaurus to find new words.

A **thesaurus** is a reference book that has synonyms (words with similar meanings) and antonyms (words with opposite meanings). You can use a thesaurus whenever you want to find more interesting words for your writing.

To look up a word you want to replace, use the thesaurus like a dictionary. Words are listed in alphabetical order. When you find your word, look at the list of words below. These are the **synonyms**, or words that have similar meanings. For example, if you looked up the word **big**, you would see the words *large*, *huge*, *bulky*, *spacious*, and *tall* listed as synonyms. The word *tiny*, which means very small, is listed as an **antonym**, or word with an opposite meaning.

**dark**
dim
shadowy
shady
murky
gloomy
bright (antonym)

**broken**
shattered
busted
wrecked
cracked
fixed (antonym)

**big**
large
huge
bulky
spacious
tall
tiny (antonym)

**squeak**
whine
yelp
creak
screech
whisper (antonym)

Copyright © Zaner-Bloser, Inc.

# Clarify

Find places to add interesting descriptive words. Use a thesaurus to find new words.

your own writing

**Now it's time for you to practice this strategy.** Read each sentence below. The word or words in bold type can be replaced with more interesting words. Choose the best synonyms for these words from the lists on page 35. Then rewrite each sentence with the new word or words.

**1.** The **big** evergreen trees make the house look **dark**.

_____

_____

_____

**2.** The shutters **squeak** on their **broken** hinges.

_____

_____

_____

**3.** The iron gate **squeaks** in the wind.

_____

_____

_____

RETURN Now go back to Sandra's work on page 62 in the Student Edition.

**Descriptive Writing** • Descriptive Paragraph

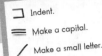

| | |
|---|---|
| ⌐ Indent. | ℓ Take out something. |
| ≡ Make a capital. | ⊙ Add a period. |
| / Make a small letter. | # New paragraph |
| ∧ Add something. | SP Spelling error |

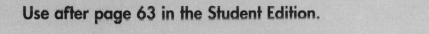

# Editing

## Proofread
Check to see that I've formed plural nouns correctly.

**Now it's time for you to practice this strategy.** Here is one writer's descriptive paragraph about a mysterious old house. Use the proofreading marks to correct the errors. Use a dictionary to help with spelling.

### Mysterious Mansion

Just looking at the mysterious old house on the hill outside

of town can give you a chill. No one has lived in that house for

more than a hundred years even on the brightest day, it is

rapped in darkness. The huge evergreen trees and bushs that

grow next to the house make it gloomier. They surround it like

ancient guards, wrapping it in a shadow of mystery. The sharp

smell of the evergreens adds to the atmosphere. The house is

falling apart because years of neglect. You can almost taste the

dust from the the crumbling walles. When the wind blows,

the shutters creak on their rickety hings. The rusted iron gate

screeches in the wind. Rough boards are nailed over the

windowes. The house seems to whisper that it holds secrets

of the passed. who is brave enough to go inside to learn

about them?

**Remember:** Use this strategy in **your own writing**

**RETURN** Now go back to Sandra's work on page 64 in the Student Edition.

# Using a  Rubric

Use this rubric to evaluate Sandra's paragraph on page 65 in your Student Edition. You may work with a partner.

## Audience

How well does the writer interest the reader in visiting an interesting place?

## Organization

Does the writer use a clear topic sentence and related detail sentences?

## Elaboration

Does the writer create a word picture that adds to the description?

## Clarification

Does the writer use interesting descriptive words?

## Conventions & Skills

Does the writer form plural nouns correctly?

your own writing

Save this rubric. Use it to check your own writing.

| Score 1 Point | Score 2 Points | Score 3 Points | Score 4 Points |
|---|---|---|---|
| ●○○○ | ●●○○ | ●●●○ | ●●●● |
| **(Novice)** | **(Apprentice)** | **(Proficient)** | **(Distinguished)** |
| There is very little information to interest the reader in visiting the place. | There is some information to create interest but not enough to make the reader want to visit the place. | There is information to create a lot of interest in the place. | The writer makes the place so interesting that the reader wants to visit it. |
| The topic sentence is missing. The details are not connected. | The topic sentence is unclear. The details are unrelated to it. | The topic sentence is clear, and most details relate to it. | The topic sentence is very clear, and all detail sentences relate to it. |
| There are no word pictures included. | There is a word picture, but it doesn't add to the description. | The writer uses a word picture that adds to the description and is also somewhat interesting. | The writer creates a word picture that adds to the description and provides very interesting information. |
| The paragraph has no descriptive words. | There are a few descriptive words. | The paragraph has many interesting descriptive words. | The paragraph is filled with descriptive words that paint vivid pictures. |
| Few plural nouns are formed correctly. | Some plural nouns are formed correctly. | Most plural nouns are formed correctly. | Plural nouns are formed correctly. |

# Prewriting

## Gather

Choose a character from a book. Jot details from the story about the character.

Remember the fairy tale about Goldilocks and the three bears? Read this new version of the old story. Then list details about the new Goldilocks on page 42 of this book.

**The Story:** *Goldilocks and the Beares*
**The Character:** Goldilocks

Once upon a time, the Beares built a nice new log house on three acres of land. There were three Beares in the family—Big Papa Beare, Mid-Sized Mama Beare, and Itty-Bitty Baby Beare. One day, the Beare family was getting ready to sit down to a meal of their favorite food—chili. The chili was too hot, so they decided to go for a walk around their property.

Just then, a young girl dressed in a Goldilocks costume knocked on their door. She was wearing a blue dress and a blond wig in a French braid. She was on her way to a costume party, and she was at the wrong house!

Nobody answered the door, so she opened it and peeked inside. She saw the table with three bowls of chili. Right away, her stomach made a hungry noise. She loved chili, too. The chili in the biggest bowl was too hot. The chili in the mid-sized bowl was too cold. The chili in the little bowl was perfect, so she sat down and ate the whole thing!

Now the girl knew she was at the wrong house. She was curious, though. She decided, "They won't mind if I just look around the house a little." In the big room she saw three chairs. She climbed into the big recliner and thought, "This is too hard." The mid-sized armchair was too soft. The small, comfy-looking rocking chair was great, so she got in it and started to rock. She rocked so hard that her wig flew off and her costume got torn and wrinkled. All of a sudden she heard a loud CRACK! and found herself on the floor. She had broken the little rocking chair.

# Prewriting

## Gather

Choose a character from a book. Jot details from the story about the character.

Now "Goldilocks" was tired, so she went looking for a place to rest. In the next room, she saw three beds. "They won't mind if I just rest for a minute," she thought. She climbed up into the biggest bed and said, "This is so lumpy!" The mid-sized bed was a waterbed and made her sick to her stomach. Then she climbed into the little bed and said, "This one is perfect." Before she knew it, she was fast asleep.

Just then, the Beares returned from their walk. They sat down to eat their chili. Big Papa Beare said, "Someone's been eating my chili." Mid-Sized Mama Beare said, "Someone's been eating my chili, too." Itty-Bitty Baby Beare looked in his bowl and exclaimed, "Hey! Someone's been eating my chili, and it's all gone!"

Then the Beares went into the big room. Right away, Big Papa Beare grumbled, "Someone's been sitting in my chair." Mid-Sized Mama Beare gasped, "Oh, look. Someone's been sitting in my chair, too." Itty-Bitty Baby Beare looked at his chair and yelled, "Hey! Someone's been sitting in my chair, and now it's busted!"

The Beares went into the next room. Big Papa Beare growled, "Someone's been lying in my bed." Mid-Sized Mama Beare muttered, "Someone's been lying in my bed, too." Itty-Bitty Baby Beare looked in his bed and shouted, "Hey! Someone's sleeping in my bed right now, and she's dressed like Goldilocks in my book!"

The shouting woke "Goldilocks" up. She sat up and said in a very grumpy voice, "What's all the noise? Can't you see that I'm trying to take a nap?" Then she looked around. She saw the Beare family standing around looking at her and let out a loud squeal. She scrambled out of bed, ran to the open window, and jumped out. The Beares never saw her again. By the way, the costume party was at the next house down the street!

# Gather
Choose a character from a book. Jot details from the story about the character.

your own writing

**Now it's time for you to practice this strategy.** Use the lines below to jot down your own notes about "Goldilocks" from the story on pages 40 and 41. Start with the list of notes on this page. Then add your own notes to the list.

## Notes About Goldilocks

wears a blond wig

is curious

eats Baby Beare's chili

says, "What's all the noise?"

_____

_____

_____

_____

_____

_____

_____

Now go back to Brandon's work on page 75 in the Student Edition.
RETURN

# Prewriting

## Organize

Make a spider map of the character. Include descriptions of how this person looks, acts, talks, and thinks.

**your own writing**

**Now it's time for you to practice this strategy.** Use the spider map below as a starting point. Use your notes from page 42 to fill in the rest of the spider map.

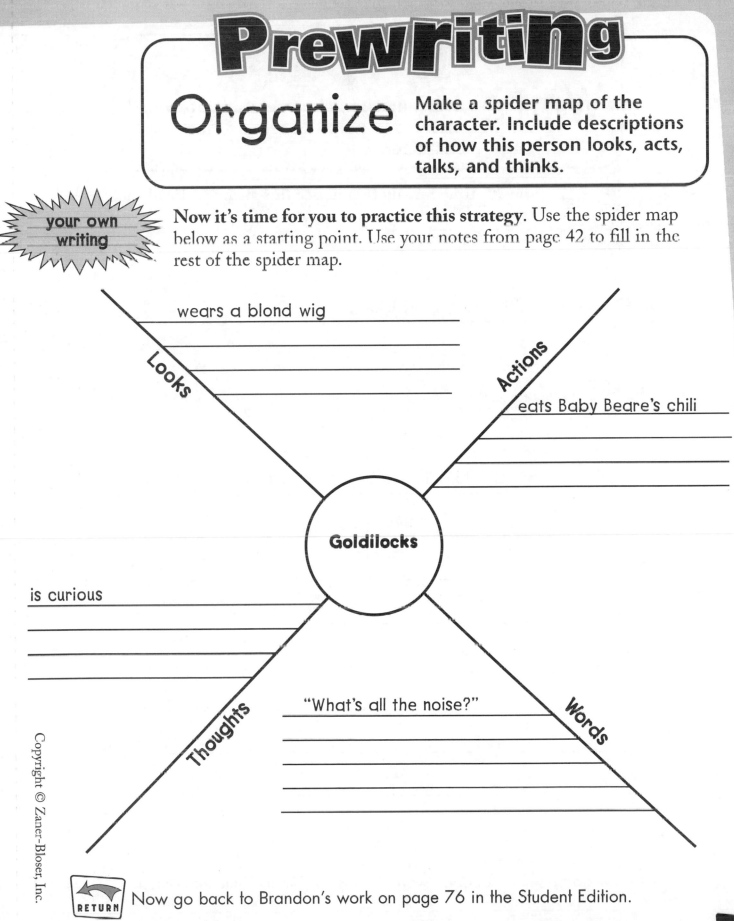

Looks

wears a blond wig

Actions

eats Baby Beare's chili

Goldilocks

is curious

Thoughts

"What's all the noise?"

Words

**RETURN** Now go back to Brandon's work on page 76 in the Student Edition.

**Descriptive Writing** • Character Sketch

43

# Drafting

## Write
Draft my character sketch. Write word pictures to help the reader "see" my character.

**your own writing**

**Now it's time for you to practice this strategy.** Read each sentence. Write a sentence that could follow it. Your sentence should help the reader "see" the character.

1. "Goldilocks" is a girl who is too curious.

_____

_____

_____

_____

2. "Goldilocks" is not very considerate of others' things.

_____

_____

_____

_____

3. "Goldilocks" has bad manners.

_____

_____

_____

_____

**RETURN** Now go back to Brandon's work on page 78 in the Student Edition.

**Descriptive Writing** • Character Sketch

# ReVising

## Elaborate
Look for places to add specific details about my character.

**your own writing**

**Now it's time for you to practice this strategy.** Read each sentence. Write two or more sentences that could follow it. Your sentences should add specific details about "Goldilocks."

1. When "Goldilocks" goes inside the house, she does whatever she wants.

_____

_____

_____

_____

_____

2. Some people might have worried about the damage they did, but not "Goldilocks."

_____

_____

_____

_____

_____

 **RETURN** Now go back to Brandon's work on page 79 in the Student Edition.

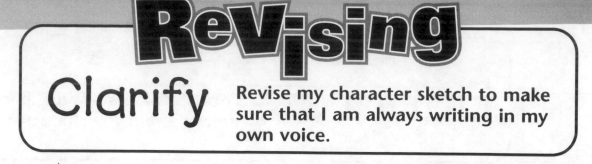

# ReVising

## Clarify

Revise my character sketch to make sure that I am always writing in my own voice.

your own writing

**Now it's time for you to practice this strategy**. Read the two paragraphs below. Both paragraphs are about the same thing, but each one is written in a different voice. Circle the words or phrases in each paragraph that help the audience "hear" the voice of the writer. Use the lines below to write this paragraph in your own voice.

"Goldilocks" is a very unusual child. She looks around the Beares' house without permission. She eats the Beares' food, and she breaks their furniture. Finally, "Goldilocks" sleeps in Baby Beare's bed until the Beares wake her up. Then she becomes frightened and runs away.

"Goldilocks" is an amazing girl. She snoops around in the Beares' house without permission. She chows down on their food, and busts up their furniture. Finally, "Goldilocks" takes a power nap in Baby Beare's bed until the Beares wake her up. Then she gets scared and makes a mad dash out the window.

_____

_____

_____

_____

_____

_____

_____

RETURN  Now go back to Brandon's work on page 80 in the Student Edition.

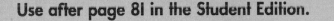

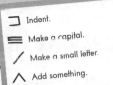

| | |
|---|---|
| ⌐ Indent. | ℓ Take out something. |
| = Make a capital. | ⊙ Add a period. |
| / Make a small letter. | # New paragraph |
| ∧ Add something. | SP Spelling error |

# Editing

# Proofread

Check that every sentence begins with a capital letter and ends with the correct punctuation mark. Check to make sure that there are no run-on sentences.

**Now it's time for you to practice this strategy.** Here is a draft of a character sketch of "Goldilocks." Use the proofreading marks to correct the errors. Use a dictionary to help with spelling.

## Goldilocks—Not an Ordinary Girl

Goldilocks is an ordinary girl dressed in a costume and a blond wig. However, this Goldilocks doesn't act like any regelar child. She is too curious she does things children shouldn't do. she knows she's in the wrong house she walks right in. She leaves Papa Beare's and Mama Beare's chili she eats up all of Baby Beare's food. She rocs in Baby Beare's chair her wig flies off her costume gets torn and wrinkled. Then she brakes Baby Bear's chair. She says, "They won't mind if I just look around the house a little." she tries out the Beares' beds and falls asleep in Baby Beare's bed. The Beares discover her, but she don't even say that she is sorry. She just jumps out of the window and gets away as fast as she can. goldilocks doesn't think what she is doing is wrong it is. Goldilocks needs to learn some manners.

**Remember:** Use this strategy in **your own writing**

Now go back to Brandon's work on page 82 in the Student Edition.

# Using a Rubric

Use this rubric to assess Brandon's character sketch on page 83 in your Student Edition. You may work with a partner.

## Audience

How well does the writer use descriptive words to help the audience picture the character?

## Organization

Does the character sketch have well-organized descriptions of the character's looks, actions, words, and thoughts?

## Elaboration

Does the writer include specific details about the character?

## Clarification

Is the writer's "voice" clear?

**your own writing**

Save this rubric. Use it to check your own writing.

## Conventions & Skills

Does each sentence begin with a capital letter and end with the correct punctuation mark? Are there any run-on sentences?

## Score 1 Point
### (Novice)

There are almost no descriptive words to help the reader picture the character.

The descriptions of the character's actions, words, thoughts, and looks are not well organized or complete.

The character sketch lacks specific details.

The writer's voice is not clear.

Many sentences do not begin with a capital letter or end with correct punctuation. There are many run-on sentences.

## Score 2 Points
### (Apprentice)

A few descriptive words help the reader imagine the character.

The descriptions of the character are somewhat organized but not always complete.

Some details are used, but they are not specific or related to the character.

The writer's voice is sometimes present, but it is not always clear.

A few sentences do not begin with a capital letter or end with correct punctuation. There are some run-on sentences.

## Score 3 Points
### (Proficient)

Some descriptive words help the reader "see" the character.

The descriptions of the character are mostly organized and nearly complete.

The writer uses many well-chosen specific details.

Most of the time the writer's voice is clear.

Only one or two sentences do not begin with a capital letter or end with correct punctuation. There are one or two run-on sentences.

## Score 4 Points
### (Distinguished)

The character is very real to the reader. The writer uses many descriptive words.

The character sketch has well-organized, complete descriptions of the character.

The character sketch is filled with excellent specific details.

The writer's voice is consistently present and clear.

Sentences begin with a capital letter and end with correct punctuation. There are no run-on sentences.

# Prewriting

## Gather

Choose two things to compare and contrast. List everything I know about each thing.

Read these two paragraphs. One is about cacti, and the other is about water lilies.

### Cacti

Cacti are mainly desert plants. They have to make the best possible use of water. When it rains, cacti take in water fast through their big root systems. They store the water in spongy layers. Then they use it very slowly. Most cacti have a thick outer layer to keep water inside. Most cacti also have sharp spines to protect them. A few creatures, such as the Gila woodpecker and the elf owl, use cacti for shelter. Many cacti have beautiful bright red or orange flowers. Some of the flowers open only at night.

### Water Lilies

Water lilies are plants that grow in shallow ponds, in slow-moving streams, and on the borders of lakes. Most water lilies have waxy leaves that keep water out. They have small roots and poorly developed layers for holding water. The leaves, or lily pads, float on top of the water. They can be big and strong enough to hold insects and frogs. Water lilies have stalks that grow underwater. They grow from stems that are buried in the mud. Many water lilies have beautiful white flowers. Some of the flowers open only at night.

# Prewriting

## Gather

Choose two things to compare and contrast. List everything I know about each thing.

**your own writing**

**Now it's your turn to practice this strategy with a different topic.** Now list everything you just learned about cacti and water lilies. Add anything else you know about those two plants.

| Cacti | Water Lilies |
| --- | --- |
| | |
| | |
| | |
| | |
| | |
| | |
| | |
| | |
| | |
| | |

**RETURN** Now go back to Miguel's work on page 95 in the Student Edition.

# Prewriting
## Organize
Use what I know to make an attribute chart.

**your own writing**

**Now it's time for you to practice this strategy.** Use the list you made on page 51 to complete this attribute chart.

| Cacti | Attribute | Water Lilies |
|---|---|---|
| | what they are | |
| | where they grow | |
| | appearance | |
| | roots | |
| | inside layers | |
| | outside layers | |
| | flowers | |
| | animals that use them | |

 Now go back to Miguel's work on page 96 in the Student Edition.

## Write
Write my essay. Begin with a compare-and-contrast lead that gets my reader's attention.

your own writing

**Now it's time for you to practice this strategy.** Look at the attribute chart you filled in on page 52. Think about what could be included in an essay on cacti and water lilies.

Write two compare-and-contrast leads that would get a reader's attention. An interesting lead is often a question or a surprising statement. An example of each one is written for you.

**1.** How can you tell the difference between a cactus and a water lily?

_____

_____

_____

_____

**2.** They may be beautiful, but the cactus and the water lily are tough survivors.

_____

_____

_____

_____

Now turn to page 54 in this notebook.

# Drafting

## Write
Write my essay. Begin with a compare-and-contrast lead that gets my reader's attention.

**your own writing**

**Now it's time for you to practice this strategy.** Use the lines below to write your own draft of a compare-and-contrast essay about cacti and water lilies.

_____

_____

_____

_____

_____

_____

_____

_____

_____

_____

_____

**RETURN** Now go back to Miguel's work on page 98 in the Student Edition.

# Revising

## Elaborate  Add examples where I need them.

**Now it's time for you to practice this strategy.** Read this compare-and-contrast paragraph.

Cacti and water lilies are alike in certain ways. Both can have very

beautiful flowers. In addition, both cacti and water lilies are used

by animals.

Read the following sentences. Cross out the three sentences that you could not use as examples in the paragraph above. Add the remaining three sentences where they belong in the compare-and-contrast paragraph above.

- My friend's mother has a cactus plant.
- Some kinds of cacti and some kinds of water lilies have flowers that bloom only at night.
- The Gila woodpecker and the elf owl make their homes in one kind of cactus.
- There is a painting of water lilies in our classroom.
- Frogs and insects can travel from one lily pad to another.
- Do not take cacti from the desert!

Remember: Use this strategy in **your own writing**

RETURN Now go back to Miguel's work on page 99 in the Student Edition.

# ReVising

## Clarify

Add signal words to make my comparisons and contrasts clear to my audience.

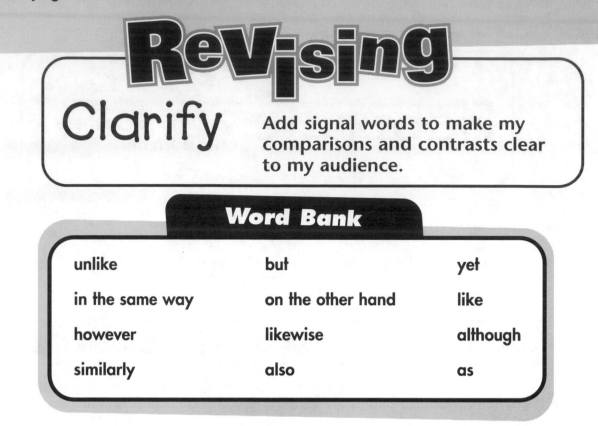

### Word Bank

| | | |
|---|---|---|
| unlike | but | yet |
| in the same way | on the other hand | like |
| however | likewise | although |
| similarly | also | as |

Fill in the chart below with the compare-and-contrast signal words from the Word Bank. If a word signals a comparison, write it under **Comparison Words**. If a word signals a contrast, write it under **Contrast Words**.

| Comparison Words | | Contrast Words | |
|---|---|---|---|
| | | | |
| | | | |
| | | | |

**Now it's time for you to practice this strategy.** Read each pair of sentences. Rewrite the sentences using signal words from the chart to show either a comparison or a contrast.

1. Most cacti grow in very hot, dry places. Water lilies grow right in the water.

_____

_____

**Expository Writing** • Compare-and-Contrast Essay

# ReVising

## Clarify

Add signal words to make my comparisons and contrasts clear to my audience.

**2.** Once a cactus gets water, it needs to hold on to it. A water lily lives in water, so it needs to keep some water out.

_____

_____

_____

**3.** The cactus has to adapt to a water problem. The water lily has to adapt to a water problem.

_____

_____

_____

**4.** The cactus gets as much water as it can through its big root system. The water lily has small roots and does not take in much water through them.

_____

_____

_____

_____

Remember: Use this strategy in your own writing

RETURN Now go back to Miguel's work on page 100 in the Student Edition.

**Expository Writing** · Compare-and-Contrast Essay

# Editing

## Proofread

Check to see that I've used homophones correctly.

⌐ Indent.
≡ Make a capital.
/ Make a small letter.
∧ Add something.
ℓ Take out something.
⊙ Add a period.
# New paragraph
SP Spelling error

**Now it's time for you to practice this strategy.** Here is a revised draft of a compare-and-contrast essay about cacti and water lilies. Use the proofreading marks to correct the errors. Use a dictionary to help with spelling.

### A Water World of Difference

Can any two plants be more different than a cactus and a water lily? Most cacti grow in deserts or in other very hot, dry places. A cactus gets water through a giant root system. it has a very thick outer layer that prevents water from evaporating. A cactus has meny spongy layers to hold a lot of water for a long time.

Unlike cacti, water lilies grow and live in water. There found in shallow ponds, in slow-moving streams, and at the edge of lakes. They're leaves, called lily pads, float in water. While a cactus has too hold in water, a water lily has to keep out some water so that air and sunlight can get in. For this reason, a water lily has a small root system. It's leaves have a waxy cover to keep the water lily from taking in extra water.

# Editing

## Proofread
Check to see that I've used homophones correctly.

| | |
|---|---|
| ⅂ Indent. | ℒ Take out something. |
| ≡ Make a capital. | ⊙ Add a period. |
| / Make a small letter. | # New paragraph |
| ∧ Add something. | SP Spelling error |

Your sure to see that both cacti and water lilies have to adapt to water. Cacti and water lilies are alike in other ways, two. Both can have very beautiful flowers. Some kinds of cacti and some kinds of water lilies have flowers that bloom only at night. Both cacti and water lilies can be used by animals. For example, the Gila woodpecker and the elf owl make there homes in one kind of cactus. Frogs and insects often rest and travel on lily pads.

Although the cactus and the water lily have many things in common, they look very different from each other. The cactus has thick leaves and sharp spines. It usually looks heavy and strong. With its pale flowers, the water lily looks delicate and fragile.

Its true that they have many differences. however, both the cactus and the water lily are amazing examples of how plants adapt to the world.

**Remember:** Use this strategy in *your own writing*

 Now go back to Miguel's work on page 102 in the Student Edition.

# Using a

Rubric

Use this rubric to assess Miguel's compare-and-contrast essay on page 103 in your Student Edition. You may work with a partner.

Audience

How well does the compare-and-contrast lead get the reader's attention?

Organization

Are the comparisons and contrasts well organized and easy to follow?

Elaboration

Do examples explain the comparisons and contrasts?

Clarification

Do signal words tell the reader that a comparison or a contrast is coming?

your own writing

Save this rubric. Use it to check your own writing.

Conventions & Skills

Are homophones used correctly?

| Score 1 Point | Score 2 Points | Score 3 Points | Score 4 Points |
|---|---|---|---|
| **(Novice)** | **(Apprentice)** | **(Proficient)** | **(Distinguished)** |
| There is no lead, or the lead does not get the reader's attention. | The essay has a compare-and-contrast lead, but it is not interesting enough. | The essay has an interesting compare-and-contrast lead. | The essay's compare-and-contrast lead makes the reader want to read more. |
| Almost no comparisons or contrasts are made. | A few comparisons and contrasts are made, but they are disorganized and difficult to follow. | Some comparisons and contrasts are made, and they are mostly organized and easy to follow. | Well-organized and easy-to-follow comparisons and contrasts are made throughout the essay. |
| There are very few examples to explain the comparisons and contrasts. | Some examples explain the comparisons and contrasts. | Examples usually explain the comparisons and contrasts. | Excellent examples explain the comparisons and contrasts throughout. |
| The essay has no signal words, or they are used incorrectly. | There are a few signal words, but they are not always appropriate or used correctly. | The writer correctly uses signal words to show that a comparison or contrast is coming. | The writer chooses excellent signal words to show relationships. |
| Few homophones are used correctly. | Some homophones are used correctly. | Most homophones are used correctly. | Homophones are used correctly. |

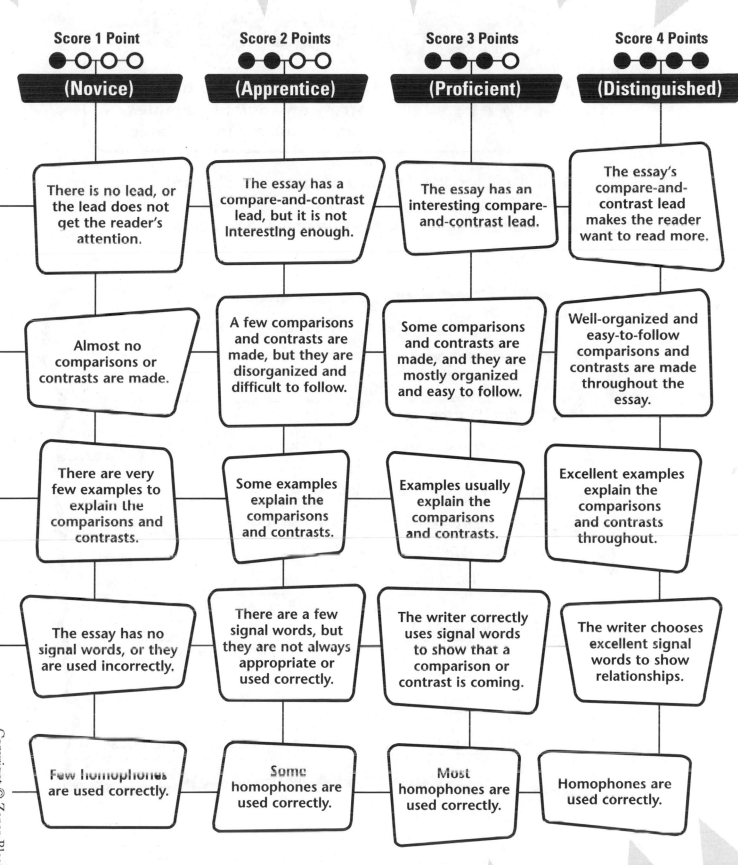

# Prewriting

## Gather
Use an encyclopedia to help me narrow my topic. Take notes from a book about my topic.

One writer skimmed an encyclopedia article about storms. She used that article to narrow her topic to one kind of storm—tornadoes. Read these notes about tornadoes that this writer took from a book on tornadoes.

### Book Notes on My Topic—Tornadoes

**dangerous storms**

- do a lot of damage
- can flatten homes
- can cut a wide strip of damage over a large area

**how tornadoes are formed**

- form when cold air meets warm air
- winds spin
- funnel clouds

**how people prepare**

- listen to radio or watch TV for information
- look for shelter
- go to lowest floor of building
- go to small room or closet in the center of the house

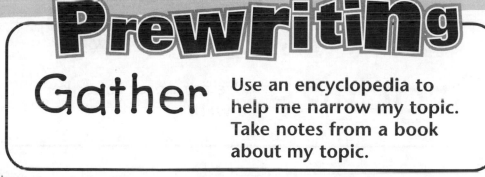

# Prewriting

## Gather

Use an encyclopedia to help me narrow my topic. Take notes from a book about my topic.

your own writing

**Now it's your turn to practice this strategy with a different topic.** Read an encyclopedia article about any topic that interests you. Use the article to help you narrow your topic to something more specific. For example, you might want to read an encyclopedia article about South America. That article could help you to narrow your topic down to something more specific, like South American rain forests.

Now find a book that has information about that specific topic. Fill in the blank with the name of your narrowed-down topic. Then take notes about it from your book.

**Book Notes on My Topic—**

_____

_____

_____

_____

_____

_____

_____

_____

Now go back to Aleka's work on page 113 in the Student Edition.

# Prewriting

## Organize
Use my notes to make a web.

Take a look at the web below. The writer used her notes on page 62 to make this web. Notice how the writer used the categories **dangerous storms, how tornadoes are formed,** and **how people prepare** as the main ideas, and then added details to each category.

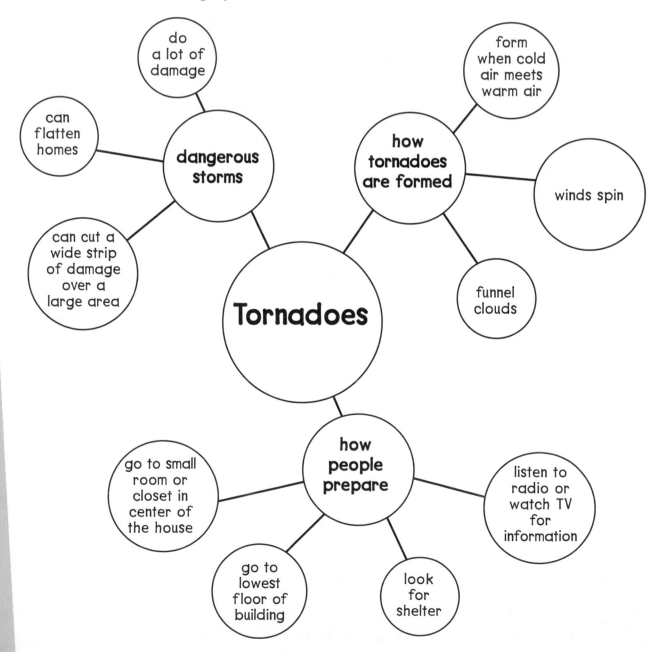

Use after page 113 in the Student Edition.

# Prewriting
## Organize
Use my notes to make a web.

your own writing

**Now it's time for you to practice this strategy.** Use your notes on page 63 to fill in the web below.

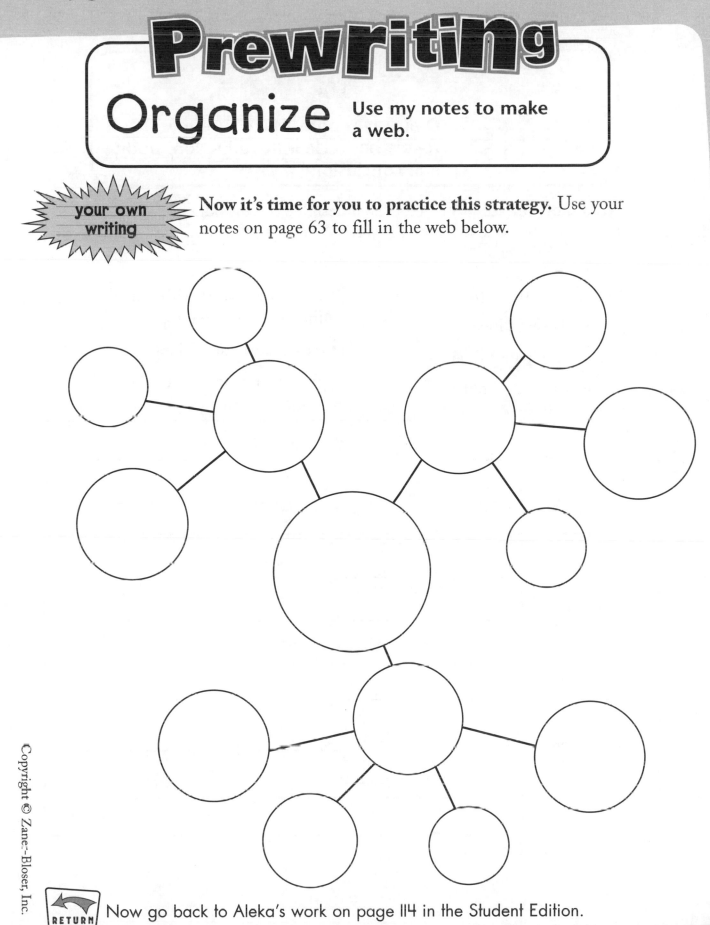

RETURN Now go back to Aleka's work on page 114 in the Student Edition.

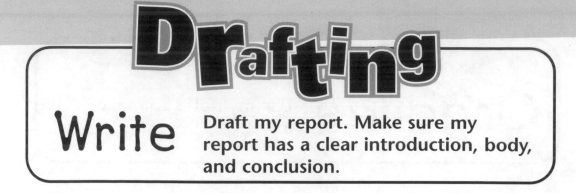

# Drafting

## Write

Draft my report. Make sure my report has a clear introduction, body, and conclusion.

Read these phrases. Which of them describe the introduction, the body, and the conclusion of a report? Write the phrases in the correct section of the chart.

- introduces the topic
- presents main ideas
- brings the paper to an end
- explains ideas about the topic

- leaves the reader with a final thought about the topic
- creates interest in the topic
- gives many facts about the topic

| Introduction | _____ |
|---|---|
| | _____ |
| Body | _____ |
| | _____ |
| | _____ |
| Conclusion | _____ |
| | _____ |

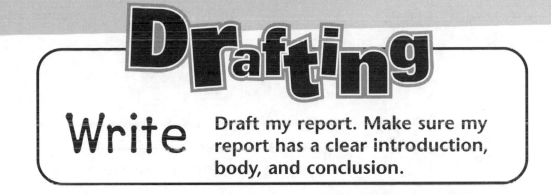

# Write

Draft my report. Make sure my report has a clear introduction, body, and conclusion.

**Now it's time for you to practice this strategy.** Use the lines below and on the next page to write a draft of your own factual report. Use the web you filled in on page 65 to draft your report. Remember to include a clear introduction, body, and conclusion.

_____

_____

_____

_____

_____

_____

_____

_____

Use after page 115 in the Student Edition.

# Drafting

**Write** Draft my report. Make sure my report has a clear introduction, body, and conclusion.

RETURN Now go back to Aleka's work on page 116 in the Student Edition.

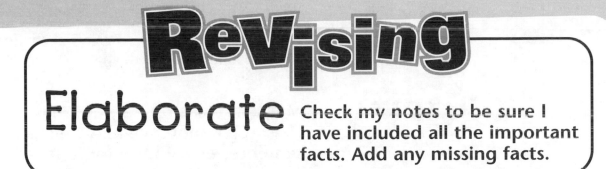

# Revising

## Elaborate

Check my notes to be sure I have included all the important facts. Add any missing facts.

**Now it's time for you to practice this strategy.** The writer checked her factual report on tornadoes. She discovered that some important facts were missing. Read the three facts below. Add these missing facts to the draft where they belong.

- Tornadoes form when a cold air mass collides with a warm air mass.
- The difference in air temperatures makes the winds spin.
- Winds in a tornado can reach speeds of more than 300 miles an hour.

Of all the storms in nature, tornadoes are some of the
most powerful.

_____

A funnel-shaped cloud then forms.

_____

_____

_____

Remember: Use this strategy in your own writing

**RETURN** Now go back to Aleka's work on page 117 in the Student Edition.

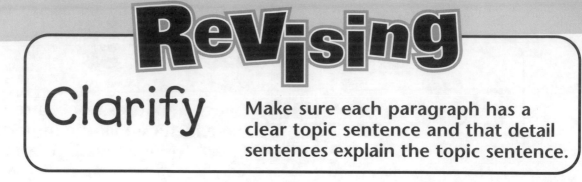

# Revising

## Clarify

Make sure each paragraph has a clear topic sentence and that detail sentences explain the topic sentence.

**Now it's time for you to practice this strategy.** In this paragraph on tornadoes, the writer starts with a clear topic sentence. Underline it.

Two of the detail sentences do not tell about that topic sentence. Cross out the two detail sentences that do not tell about the topic sentence. You will see some mistakes. You can correct them now or wait until later.

People who live in places where tornadoes happen know what to do. They listen to the radio or watch television for tornado warnings. My cousin saw an excellent program on tornadoes. when people hear a tornado warning, they find shelter. They go to the lowist floor of the nearest building or a small room or a closet near the center of the building. A new home may have lots of closets in it.

**Remember:**
Use this strategy in *your own writing*

Now go back to Aleka's work on page 118 in the Student Edition.

| | |
|---|---|
| ⌐ Indent. | ℓ Take out something. |
| = Make a capital. | ⊙ Add a period. |
| / Make a small letter. | �# New paragraph |
| ∧ Add something. | SP Spelling error |

# Editing
# Proofread
**Check that capital letters are used correctly.**

**Now it's time for you to practice this strategy.** Here is a revised draft of one writer's factual report about tornadoes. Use the proofreading marks to correct the errors. Use a dictionary to help with spelling.

Of all the storms in nature, Tornadoes are some of the most powerful. Tornadoes form when a cold air mass collides with a warm air mass. The difference in air temperatures makes the winds spin. A funnel-shaped cloud then forms. Winds in a tornado can reach speeds of more than 300 miles an hour.

Tornadoes can do a lot of damage. They can flatten Homes and cut a wide strip of damage over a large area. Tornadoes are also unusual they may destroy one house but leave the house next door untouched.

People who live in places where tornadoes happen know what to do. they listen to the radio or watch television for tornado warnings. when people hear a tornado warning, they find shelter. They go to the lowist floor of the nearest building or a small room or a closet near the center of the building.

living with tornadoes is not as dangrous as it once was. It is easier to learn when a tornado is coming than it use to be. Today, people can deal better with these terribel storms.

*Remember: Use this strategy in your own writing*

Now go back to Aleka's paper on page 120 in the Student Edition.

# Using a

Use this rubric to assess Aleka's essay on page 121 in your Student Edition. You may work with a partner.

**Audience**

Does the writer focus on the most interesting information about the topic?

**Organization**

Does the report have an introduction, body, and conclusion?

**Elaboration**

Does the report have enough important facts?

**Clarification**

Does every paragraph have a topic sentence? Do all the detail sentences explain the topic sentence?

**your own writing**

Save this rubric. Use it to check your own writing.

**Conventions & Skills**

Are capital letters used correctly?

**Score 1 Point**
●○○○
**(Novice)**

There is no interesting information about the topic.

The report does not have a clear introduction, body, or conclusion.

No important facts are included.

Most paragraphs do not have a topic sentence.

The report has many errors with capital letters.

**Score 2 Points**
●●○○
**(Apprentice)**

There is some interesting information about the topic.

The report has a body but no introduction or conclusion.

A few important facts are included.

Most paragraphs have a topic sentence, but detail sentences do not explain it.

A few capital letters are used correctly.

**Score 3 Points**
●●●○
**(Proficient)**

There is interesting information about the topic.

The report has a body and a clear introduction or conclusion.

Some important facts are included.

Most paragraphs have a topic sentence with detail sentences that explain it.

Most capital letters are used correctly.

**Score 4 Points**
●●●●
**(Distinguished)**

The report is focused on a lot of interesting information about the topic.

The report has a clear introduction, body, and conclusion.

The report is complete. It contains many important facts.

Every paragraph has a topic sentence with detail sentences that explain it.

All capital letters are used correctly.

# Prewriting
## Gather   Decide on the problem.

**your own writing**

**Now it's time to practice this strategy with different topics.** Look at this picture. The characters are Adam's mom, Adam, Adam's cousin Josh, and Adam's dog, whose name is Taffy. How would you describe the setting? What kind of adventure do you think these characters could be having? What might be the problem? Write your ideas on the lines below.

**Problem**

_____

_____

_____

_____

_____

**RETURN** Now go back to Megan's work on page 133 in the Student Edition.

# Prewriting
## Organize
Make a story map to plan my story.

**your own writing**

**Now it's time for you to practice this strategy.** Use the illustration on page 74 and your notes to fill in the story map below.

| |
|---|
| **Setting:** |
| Where: |
| When: |
| **Characters:** |
| **Problem:** |
| **Plot/Events:** |
| **Ending:** |

Now go back to Megan's work on page 134 in the Student Edition.

**Narrative Writing** • Adventure Story

# Drafting

## Write
Build my story to a climax and then wrap it up.

**your own writing**

**Now it's time for you to practice this strategy.** An adventure story usually builds slowly. On the lines below and on the next page, draft your adventure story. Use the story map on page 75 as a guide to write your draft. Remember that your story should build to a climax, or the most important part of the story. You can create the "build-up" in your draft by adding details that show excitement or suspense. Here are some words that may help you do this.

### Word Bank

| | | |
|---|---|---|
| whispered | shouting | sharply |
| into nowhere | tensely | breathless |
| suddenly | danger | terrified |
| somehow | bolted | chasing |

**Narrative Writing • Adventure Story**

Use after page 135 in the Student Edition.

# Drafting

## Write

**Build my story to a climax and then wrap it up.**



RETURN Now go back to Megan's work on page 136 in the Student Edition.

# ReVising
## Elaborate
Add dialogue to make my story more exciting.

**Now it's time for you to practice this strategy.** Read each sentence below. Rewrite each one as a direct quotation. Be sure to add quotation marks to direct quotations. The first one is done for you. Remember to use dialogue in your own draft to make your story more exciting.

1. She said that Taffy was headed straight for Sunset Overlook.

   "Taffy is headed straight for Sunset Overlook," she
   explained quickly.

2. Josh said that he was really worried about Taffy.

   _____

   _____

3. I told everyone that the cliff dropped into nowhere.

   _____

   _____

4. She said that there was a fence but that an excited little dog could run right under it.

   _____

   _____

Remember: Use this strategy in your own writing

RETURN Now go back to Megan's work on page 137 in the Student Edition.

**78**   **Narrative Writing** • Adventure Story

# Revising

## Clarify
Add words and phrases that build suspense and excitement.

Read a part of what another writer wrote based on the picture on page 74. Then cross out and replace the words in bold type in the story with the words from the Word Bank that build more suspense and excitement. Don't forget to use words like this that build suspense and excitement in your own adventure story.

### Word Bank

| | | |
|---|---|---|
| caught sight of | grabbed | snatched up |
| took off | raced | only a few feet from |

We **went** to the grill. Josh **got** a plate filled with hot dogs.

_____

I **got** a plate filled with hamburgers. We **went** after Taffy

_____

in the direction of Sunset Overlook.

_____

By the time we **saw** her again, she was **near** the cliff.

_____

"Taffy! Taffy!" we called.

_____

Remember: Use this strategy in **your own writing**

Now go back to Megan's work on page 138 in the Student Edition.

| Indent. | Take out something. |
|---|---|
| Make a capital. | Add a period. |
| Make a small letter. | New paragraph |
| Add something. | Spelling error |

# Editing
# Proofread
Check that direct quotations have been punctuated correctly.

**Now it's your turn to practice this strategy.** Here is a revised draft of one writer's adventure story about Taffy. Use the proofreading marks to correct the errors. Use a dictionary to help with spelling.

### Taffy's Picnic

When we went to Thatcher State Park for a picnic on a windy fall day, we brung our dog, Taffy. She is a good dog, but when she gets loose, she likes to run.

The grownups were all busy at the grill. Suddenly, somehow, Taffy got loose. Mom and I started searching for her. We finally spotted her in a big field. As I ran toward her, I called, "Taffy! Taffy!" Mom whispered tensely, "Ssssh, Adam!"

Surprised, I asked, What's the matter

When I saw the look on Mom's face, I didn't say another word. My friend Josh, though, hadn't heard her. He started "shouting and running" after Taffy. When Taffy saw him, she bolted in the opposite direkshun. Mom knew what would happen. "Taffy is headed for Sunset Overlook," she explained quickly.

Josh and me looked at each other. "Oh, no!" shouted Josh.

I cried, "That cliff drops down into nowhere!"

Mom tried to reassure us. "There is a fence," she said.

**Narrative Writing** • Adventure Story

| ⌐ Indent. | 𝓁 Take out something. |
| ≡ Make a capital. | ⊙ Add a period. |
| / Make a small letter. | ⌗ New paragraph |
| ∧ Add something. | SP Spelling error |

# Editing

## Proofread
Check that direct quotations have been punctuated correctly.

"An excited little dog could run right under it, though."

Josh and I looked at each other again.

"Hot dogs!" Josh cried.

"Hamburgers!" I yelled.

We raced to the grill. Josh grabbed a plate filled with hot dogs. I snatched up a plate filled with hamburgers. We took off after Taffy. By the time we caught sight of her again, she was only a few feet from the cliff. "Taffy! Taffy!" we called.

At that moment, the wind picked up. The wind blew the smell of hot dogs and hamburgers in Taffy's direction

Taffy stoped short. as Josh and I walked slowly toward her, she made a quick turn toward us. We held in our breath. Taffy came running as we put both plates on the ground. Soon Taffy was siting in the middle of a pile of hot dogs and hamburgers, taking happy bites from our lunch.

Enjoy yourself, Taffy, said Josh. "You'll never have a picnic like this again in your whole life." I had to laugh.

**Remember:** Use this strategy in **your own writing**

Now go back to Megan's work on page 140 in the Student Edition.

# Using a

Use this rubric to evaluate Megan's adventure story on pages 141–143 in your Student Edition. You may work with a partner.

Is the adventure story appropriate for the intended audience? Can readers relate to the characters and the problem?

Does the story have a setting, a problem, and an ending?

How well does the writer use dialogue to make the story more exciting?

Save this rubric. Use it to check your own writing.

How well does the writer use words and phrases to build suspense and excitement?

Are all the direct quotations punctuated correctly?

| Score 1 Point | Score 2 Points | Score 3 Points | Score 4 Points |
|---|---|---|---|
| ●○○○ **(Novice)** | ●●○○ **(Apprentice)** | ●●●○ **(Proficient)** | ●●●● **(Distinguished)** |

| | | | |
|---|---|---|---|
| The story is not appropriate for the intended audience. Most readers probably won't relate to the characters or the problem. | Some parts of the story are appropriate for the intended audience. Readers may relate to the characters or the problem, but not both. | Most events in the story are appropriate for the intended audience. Readers will probably relate to the characters and the problem. | The adventure is appropriate for the intended audience. The characters and the problem are completely believable to readers. |
| The story is missing a setting, a problem, and an ending. | The story is missing two of the three important pieces. | The story includes most of the important pieces. | The story has a clear setting, a problem, and an ending. |
| There is no dialogue. | The writer uses dialogue, but it does not add excitement to the story. | The writer occasionally uses dialogue to make the story exciting. | There is enough dialogue to make the story come alive with excitement. |
| The writer does not use words or phrases that build suspense and excitement. | The writer uses one or two words or phrases that build suspense and excitement. | The writer uses many words or phrases that build suspense and excitement. | The writer chooses words that build a lot of suspense and excitement. |
| There are no direct quotations to punctuate. | Some of the direct quotations are punctuated correctly. | Most of the direct quotations are punctuated correctly. | All of the direct quotations are punctuated correctly. |

# Prewriting

## Gather

Think about things that have happened to me. Make a list of people and events.

Here's a list of people and events that one writer remembered from her own life.

**Characters**

- me (Lindsay)    • Kylee    • my brother Ken

**Events**

- My twin brother and I started at a new school.

- He was really happy about it.

- I hated the idea.

- The first day there, I met Kylee.

- Now I have a best friend.

**Now it's your turn to practice this strategy with a different topic.** Think about something that happened in your own life. Write down the people and events on the lines below.

**Characters**

_____

_____

**Events**

_____

_____

_____

# Prewriting

## Gather

**Think about things that have happened to me. Make a list of people and events.**

Read how this writer turned her list of people and events into a list of people and events for her contemporary story.

### Characters

- Courtney

- Ian, Courtney's twin brother

### Events

- Courtney and Ian's family move from the city to the country.

- Ian is happy about the move.

- Courtney is not happy about it.

- As they're moving into the new house, Courtney meets Caroline.

- Now Courtney has a new friend.

**Now it's time for you to practice this strategy.** Use the list you wrote on page 84 to make a list of characters and events for your own contemporary story.

### Characters

_____

_____

### Events

_____

_____

_____

_____

Now go back to Charles's work on page 154 in the Student Edition.

# Prewriting
## Organize

Make a character chart to plan out each main character.

Here are the writer's character charts for Ian and Courtney.

| Character: Ian | |
| --- | --- |
| **How He Acts** | **How He Feels** |
| packs his room fast<br><br>helps the movers load up the van<br><br>shouts "Hooray!" | excited to move<br><br>looks foward to living in the country<br><br>happy |

| Character: Courtney | |
| --- | --- |
| **How She Acts** | **How She Feels** |
| says she's not getting out of bed<br><br>moves slowly<br><br>cries in the car | not happy about the move<br><br>doesn't want to live in the country<br><br>is going to miss her best friend<br><br>happy when she meets Caroline |

# Prewriting

## Organize
Make a character chart to plan out each main character.

**your own writing**

**Now it's time for you to practice this strategy.** Make character charts for the two main characters in your contemporary story.

**First Character:**

| How He or She Acts | How He or She Feels |
|---|---|
|  |  |
|  |  |
|  |  |
|  |  |
|  |  |
|  |  |

**Second Character:**

| How He or She Acts | How He or She Feels |
|---|---|
|  |  |
|  |  |
|  |  |
|  |  |
|  |  |

**RETURN** Now go back to Charles's work on page 156 in the Student Edition.

# Drafting

## Write

**Draft a story that makes the conflict clear and interesting.**

*your own writing*

**Now it's time for you to practice this strategy.** Use the lines below to draft your own contemporary story. Remember to give your story a clear and interesting conflict.

_____

_____

_____

_____

_____

_____

_____

_____

_____

_____

_____

_____

# Drafting

## Write    Draft a story that makes the conflict clear and interesting.

_____

_____

_____

_____

_____

_____

_____

_____

_____

_____

_____

_____

RETURN  Now go back to Charles's work on page 158 in the Student Edition.

# Revising
## Elaborate
**Look for places to add details about my characters.**

**Now it's time for you to practice this strategy.** The writer needs some details about the character to make the story more interest-ing. Read the details below. Write them in the draft where you think they belong.

- She did not want to move to the country.
- She had never wanted this day to arrive.
- Kelly and she had gone to school together all their lives.

_____

Courtney was Ian's twin. "I'm not getting out of bed, " she

_____

announced. All Courtney could think about was her friend,

_____

Kelly.

_____

_____

_____

_____

_____

**Remember:** Use this strategy in **your own writing**

RETURN Now go back to Charles's work on page 159 in the Student Edition.

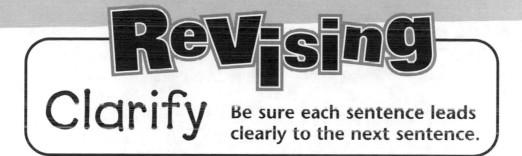

# ReVising

## Clarify

Be sure each sentence leads clearly to the next sentence.

**Now it's time for you to practice this strategy.** Read this part of the story about Courtney and Ian. Move two sentences so that each sentence leads more clearly to the next sentence. Remember to move one sentence in each paragraph.

As Courtney walked toward the house, she saw a girl her age

run across the yard toward her. "I've been waiting my whole

life for someone like you to move near my family and I. Come

visit as soon as you get settled!" She pointed to her house down

the road. "Hi, I'm Caroline!" the girl said.

"You can go now, Courtney," he said. "We'll start

unpacking." Courtney's dad heard Caroline.

Remember:
Use this strategy in
your own
writing

Now go back to Charles's work on page 160 in the Student Edition.

# Editing

## Proofread

**Check that all pronouns are used correctly.**

| | |
|---|---|
| ⌐ Indent. | ℓ Take out something. |
| ≡ Make a capital. | ⊙ Add a period. |
| / Make a small letter. | # New paragraph |
| ∧ Add something. | SP Spelling error |

**Now it's time for you to practice this strategy.** Here is a revised draft of the story about the twins who move to the country. Use the proofreading marks to correct the errors. Use a dictionary to help with spelling.

### Moving Out and Moving On

"Time to get up! Today's the day!" Mom shouted. It was moving day. The family was moving from a city apartment to a country house neer a lake.

Ian answered right away, "I m coming!" He nearly leaped out of bed. He had packed up his room days before. He couldn't wait to help the movers load the van. All Ian could think about was playing in the feilds and swimming in the lake. Maybe Dad would even build a tree house for he and his friends.

Courtney was Ian's twin. She did not want to move to the country. "I'm not getting out of bed she announced. She had never wanted this day to arrive. All Courtney could think about was her best freind, Kelly. Kelly and her had gone to school together all their lives.

At last, the van was loaded. The movers drove away. The family followed in the car. After an hour, they arrived at

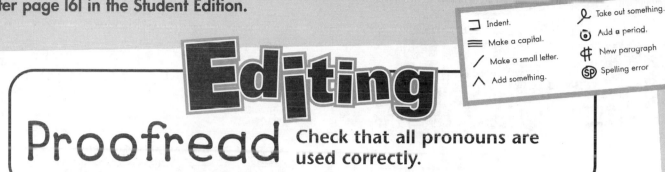

# Editing

## Proofread

Check that all pronouns are used correctly.

their new home. "Hooray!" shouted Ian. Courtney had to drie her eyes before she stepped out of the car. She said nuthing.

As Courtney walked toward the house, she saw a girl her age run across the yard toward her. "Hi, I'm Caroline!" the girl said. "I've been waiting my whole life for someone like you to move near my family and I! Come visit as soon as you get settled!" She pointed to her house down the road.

Courtney's dad heard Caroline. "You can go now, Courtney," he said. "We'll start unpacking."

Courtney went with Caroline. Soon she found out that Caroline liked shopping in the city, Computers, and indoor games. Her and Courtney discovered that they both really liked to play chess. Best of all, Caroline wanted to be Courtney's friend. Maybe, Courtney thought, Caroline and me can visit Kelly in the City, and then Kelly can spend a week with us in the country. Courtney decided she could have everything!

Remember:
Use this strategy in
your own
writing

RETURN Now go back to Charles's work on page 162 in the Student Edition.

# Using a

Use this rubric to score Charles's contemporary story on page 163 in your Student Edition. You may work with a partner.

Does the writer make the conflict clear and interesting to the reader?

Does the writer organize the plot of the story around the actions of the characters?

**Elaboration**

Does the writer add to the story's interest by including details about the characters?

Does each sentence lead clearly to the next sentence?

Save this rubric. Use it to check your own writing.

Are pronouns used correctly?

## Score 1 Point
### (Novice)

The story has no conflict.

There is no plot.

There are no details about the characters.

The story is confusing because the sentences do not lead into each other in a clear way.

Very few pronouns are used correctly.

## Score 2 Points
### (Apprentice)

The conflict is confusing or not interesting to the reader.

The plot sometimes is organized around the actions of the characters.

There are a few details about the characters.

Some sentences do not lead clearly to the next sentence, so parts of the story are unclear.

Some pronouns are used correctly.

## Score 3 Points
### (Proficient)

The conflict is mostly clear, but it could be more interesting to the reader.

Most of the time, the plot is organized around the actions of the characters.

The writer includes some details about the characters.

Most sentences lead clearly to the next sentence.

Most pronouns are used correctly.

## Score 4 Points
### (Distinguished)

There is a conflict that is interesting for the reader.

The writer develops the story around the actions of the characters.

There are many details about the characters.

The sentences are all in a clear and correct order.

All pronouns are used correctly.

# Gather
**Decide what my opinion is. List reasons to support my opinion.**

One student decided to write a persuasive essay about recycling. Read what she wrote about the topic, her opinion, and her reasons.

---

**Topic:** The city should have a free recycling program.

**My Opinion:** I'm for it.

**Reasons to Support My Opinion:**
- Other cities near us have free recycling services.
- Recycling is important for the environment.
- More people will recycle if the city makes the service available and free.
- Recycling programs can pay for themselves.
- We can show that our city keeps up with the times.

---

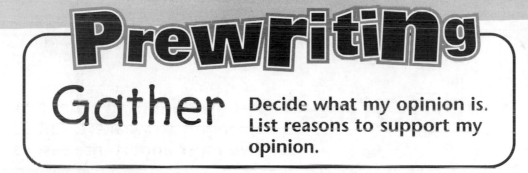

# Gather

Decide what my opinion is. List reasons to support my opinion.

**Now it's your turn to practice this strategy with different topics.** Think of a topic about which you have strong feelings. Write the topic below. Next, tell which side of the issue you are on. Then give your reasons.

**Topic:**

**My Opinion:**

_____

_____

**Reasons to Support My Opinion:**

1. _____

_____

2. _____

_____

3. _____

_____

4. _____

_____

5. _____

Now go back to Jasmine's work on page 175 in the Student Edition.

**Persuasive Writing** • Persuasive Essay

# Prewriting

## Organize

Put my reasons in order from strongest to weakest. Choose the two most important reasons.

The student writing about recycling used an order-of-importance organizer to put her reasons in order from most important to least important.

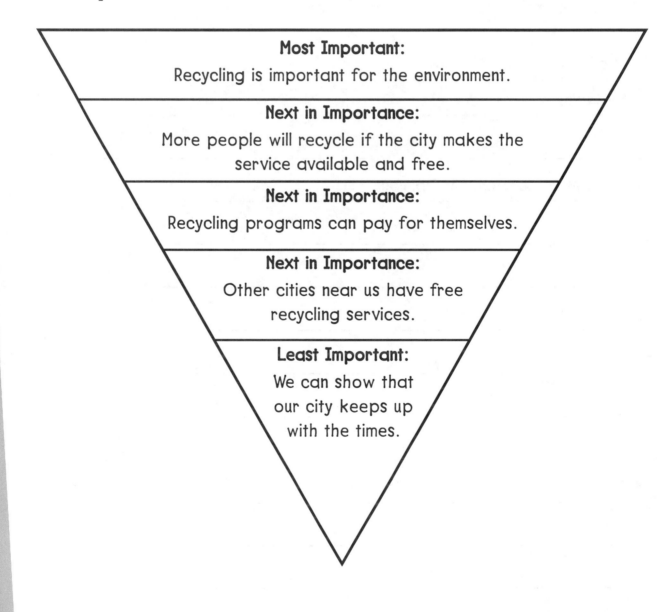

**Most Important:**
Recycling is important for the environment.

**Next in Importance:**
More people will recycle if the city makes the service available and free.

**Next in Importance:**
Recycling programs can pay for themselves.

**Next in Importance:**
Other cities near us have free recycling services.

**Least Important:**
We can show that our city keeps up with the times.

**Persuasive Writing** • Persuasive Essay

# Prewriting

## Organize

Put my reasons in order from strongest to weakest. Choose the two most important reasons.

your own writing

**Now it's time for you to practice this strategy.** Look back at the reasons you wrote on page 97. Write them in the order-of-importance organizer below. Order them from most important to least important.

Most Important:

Next in Importance:

Next in Importance:

Next in Importance:

Least Important:

RETURN Now go back to Jasmine's work on page 176 in the Student Edition.

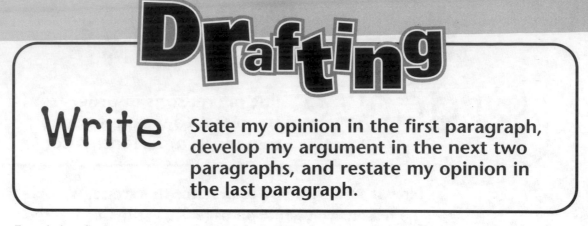

# Drafting

## Write

State my opinion in the first paragraph, develop my argument in the next two paragraphs, and restate my opinion in the last paragraph.

Look back at page 96 of this book. Find the writer's opinion about recycling. Then look at her order-of-importance organizer on page 98 to find her most important and second most important reason.

On the lines below, write the first sentence of each paragraph of a persuasive essay about recycling. The introduction should include the opinion. The next paragraph should present the more important of the two reasons. The next paragraph should present the second reason. The conclusion should restate the opinion in different words.

**First sentence of introduction:**

_____

_____

**First sentence of next paragraph:**

_____

_____

**First sentence of next paragraph:**

_____

_____

**First sentence of conclusion:**

_____

_____

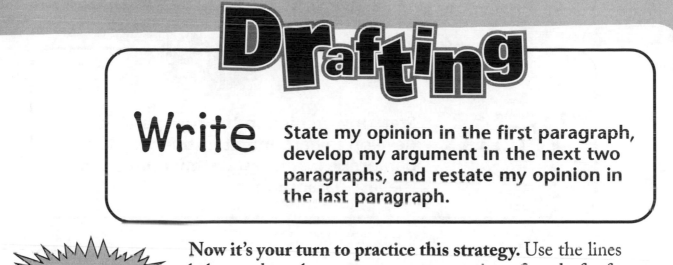

# Drafting

## Write

State my opinion in the first paragraph, develop my argument in the next two paragraphs, and restate my opinion in the last paragraph.

your own writing

**Now it's your turn to practice this strategy.** Use the lines below and on the next two pages to write a first draft of your own persuasive essay. Use the topic and reasons you wrote on page 97 and the order-of-importance organizer you filled in on page 99.

_____

_____

_____

_____

_____

_____

_____

_____

_____

_____

_____

_____

## Write

State my opinion in the first paragraph, develop my argument in the next two paragraphs, and restate my opinion in the last paragraph.

_____

_____

_____

_____

_____

_____

_____

_____

_____

_____

_____

_____

_____

_____

# Drafting

## Write

State my opinion in the first paragraph, develop my argument in the next two paragraphs, and restate my opinion in the last paragraph.

_____

_____

_____

_____

_____

_____

_____

_____

_____

_____

_____

_____

_____

_____

_____

RETURN Now go back to Jasmine's work on page 180 in the Student Edition.

# ReVising

## Elaborate
Add details and examples to make my argument stronger.

The writer of the recycling essay asked a friend to read her paper. When the friend disagreed on some points, the writer decided to make her argument stronger. Here are the details and examples the writer wants to add.

• The landfill gets used up, and then we need another one.

• We could recycle aluminum soda cans, aluminum foil, and aluminum frozen-food trays.

• People could recycle their newspapers, notebook paper, and paper cups.

**Now it's your turn to practice this strategy.** Add the writer's details and examples to strengthen the argument.

You should know, though, that most trash in a landfill does not

_____

break down. With a recycling program, a lot of our trash could

_____

be recycled. It would be well to recycle glass and metals. Most of

_____

us could recycle aluminum, for example. Paper could also be

_____

recycled. Many types of plastic could be recycled, too.

**Remember:** Use this strategy in *your own writing*

 Now go back to Jasmine's work on page 181 in the Student Edition.

**Persuasive Writing** • Persuasive Essay

# ReVising

## Clarify

Check for loaded words.
Replace them.

**Now it's time for you to practice this strategy.** Read this paragraph from the persuasive essay on recycling. The words and phrases in bold type are examples of loaded words. Cross them out, and replace them with less emotional words. You may use words from the **Word Bank** or come up with your own.

### Word Bank

| do the same | cleaner |
|---|---|
| some | workable |

Earth is the only home we have. **If they have any sense,** cities

understand this. They already have well, **life-saving** programs

in place which are free to the public. Our city should **wake up.**

As a result, more people will recycle. Our planet will be

**less of a dump,** and we will be proud of our city.

Remember:
Use this strategy in your own writing

Now go back to Jasmine's work on page 182 in the Student Edition.

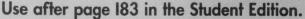

# Editing

## Proofread Check that adjectives and adverbs are used correctly.

**Now it's your turn to practice this strategy.** Here is a revised draft of the persuasive essay about recycling. Use the proofreading marks to correct the errors. Use a dictionary to help with spelling.

### Recycling for Everyone

Our city is a great place. It is cleanly, and people are friendly. One thing we need, though, is a free recycling service. The city should provide this service

Recycling is important for the environment. Most of our city's garbage gets buried in an underground landfill. You should know, though, that most trash in a landfill does not break down. The landfill gets used up, and then we need another one. With a recycling program, a lot of our trash could be recycled. It would be well to recycle glass and metals. Most of us could recycle aluminum, for example. We could recycle aluminum soda cans, aluminum foil, and aluminum frozen-food trayes. Paper could also be recycled. People could recycle their newspapers, notebook paper, and paper cuppes. Many types of plastic could be recycled, too.

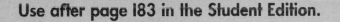

# Editing

| ⌐ | Indent. | ℓ | Take out something. |
| ≡ | Make a capital. | ⊙ | Add a period. |
| / | Make a small letter. | # | New paragraph |
| ∧ | Add something. | SP | Spelling error |

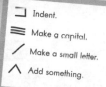

## Proofread Check that adjectives and adverbs are used correctly.

If the city supports free recycling, more people will recycle. Recycling takes time and effort. People have to separate there trash. They have to wash out containers. This stops some people from recycling or from recycling regular. Also, trash services are chargeing an extra fee for recycling. people who want to recycle must pay for it. When people have to pay, this stops even more of them from recycling. The city should pay for recycling, and it should pick up items that people put in front of their homes. If people can recycle easy, more people will do it. They will also do the job good and thorough.

Earth is the only home we have. Some cities understand this. They already have well, workable programs in place which are free to the public. Our city should do the same. As a result, more people will recycle. Our planet will be cleaner, and we will be proud of our city and ourselves.

Remember: Use this strategy in your own writing

Now go back to Jasmine's work on page 184 in the Student Edition.

# Using a Rubric

Use this rubric to evaluate Jasmine's essay on pages 185–187 in your Student Edition. You may work with a partner.

## Audience

Does the writer state an opinion, develop the argument, and restate the opinion so that it's clear to the readers?

## Organization

Does the writer organize the essay around at least two important reasons that develop the argument for his or her opinion? Does the writer use two paragraphs to do this?

## Elaboration

Does the writer give details and examples to make a strong argument?

## Clarification

Does the writer avoid using loaded words?

### your own writing

Save this rubric. Use it to check your own writing.

## Conventions & Skills

Does the writer use adjectives and adverbs correctly?

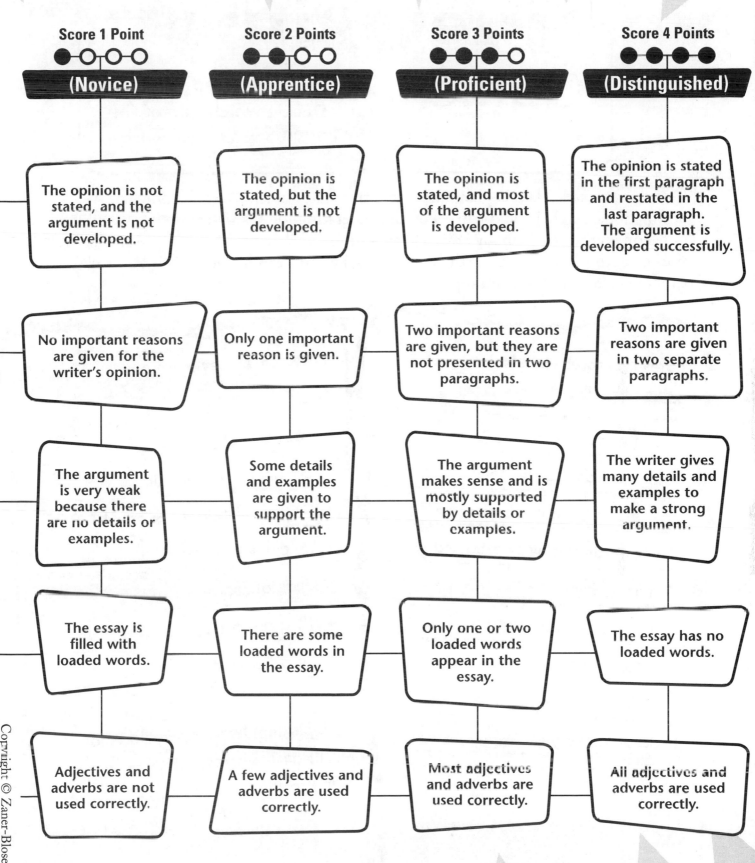

## Score 1 Point
### (Novice)

The opinion is not stated, and the argument is not developed.

No important reasons are given for the writer's opinion.

The argument is very weak because there are no details or examples.

The essay is filled with loaded words.

Adjectives and adverbs are not used correctly.

## Score 2 Points
### (Apprentice)

The opinion is stated, but the argument is not developed.

Only one important reason is given.

Some details and examples are given to support the argument.

There are some loaded words in the essay.

A few adjectives and adverbs are used correctly.

## Score 3 Points
### (Proficient)

The opinion is stated, and most of the argument is developed.

Two important reasons are given, but they are not presented in two paragraphs.

The argument makes sense and is mostly supported by details or examples.

Only one or two loaded words appear in the essay.

Most adjectives and adverbs are used correctly.

## Score 4 Points
### (Distinguished)

The opinion is stated in the first paragraph and restated in the last paragraph. The argument is developed successfully.

Two important reasons are given in two separate paragraphs.

The writer gives many details and examples to make a strong argument.

The essay has no loaded words.

All adjectives and adverbs are used correctly.

**Persuasive Writing** • Persuasive Essay

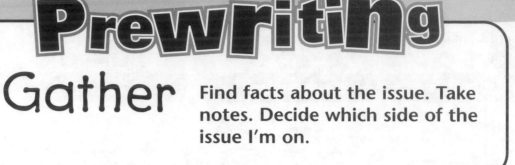

# Prewriting

## Gather

Find facts about the issue. Take notes. Decide which side of the issue I'm on.

One fourth grade class is planning a field trip. The students have a choice of two destinations for their field trip—Powell Planetarium or Tracey Mountain. Read the notes one writer took about Powell Planetarium and Tracey Mountain from the Web sites of both places. He used the facts he learned to form his opinion that his class should go to Tracey Mountain.

**Notes on Powell Planetarium**

**Facts**

- It has just one show, "Night Lights," during the school day. The "Space Laser" spectacular is shown on Friday and Saturday nights only.

- The only exhibit right now is "Mars: The Red Planet." Other exhibit halls won't open until later in the year.

**Notes on Tracey Mountain**

**Facts**

- We can get great exercise climbing the mountain.

- Crisp mountain air is good for us.

- We can learn about different kinds of plants.

- It's a great chance to learn to use a compass.

**My Opinion:** Our class would enjoy hiking on Tracey Mountain more than going to the Powell Planetarium.

**Persuasive Writing** • Friendly Letter

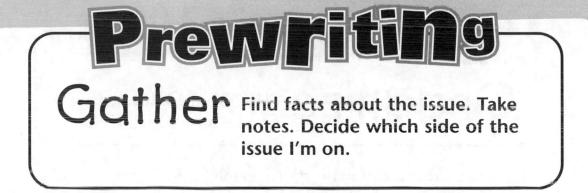

# Prewriting

## Gather
Find facts about the issue. Take notes. Decide which side of the issue I'm on.

**your own writing**

**Now it's your turn to practice this strategy.** Read about two places to visit, or research two other topics on the Internet, in the newspaper, or in a magazine. Have an adult help you to use the Internet. Take notes about both topics. Decide which side of the issue you're on.

Notes on: _____

Facts: _____

_____

_____

_____

Notes on: _____

Facts: _____

_____

_____

_____

My Opinion: _____

_____

_____

**RETURN** Now go back to Van's work on page 197 in the Student Edition.

# PreWRiting
# Organize   Use what I know to make a network tree.

The writer created this network tree graphic organizer to organize his notes. He put his opinion at the top. The two reasons for his opinion are in the next two circles. Facts that support his reasons are in the next set of circles.

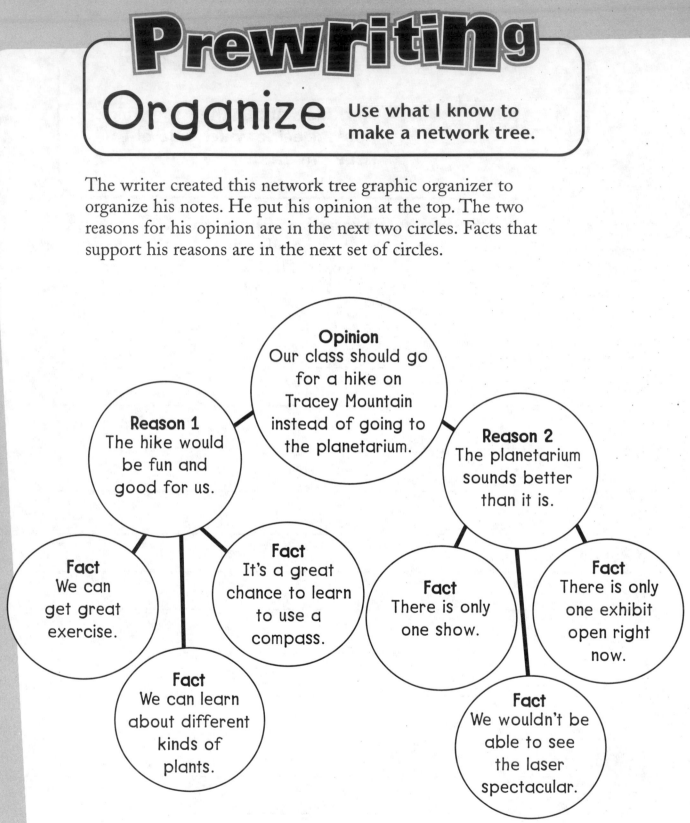

**Opinion**
Our class should go for a hike on Tracey Mountain instead of going to the planetarium.

**Reason 1**
The hike would be fun and good for us.

**Reason 2**
The planetarium sounds better than it is.

**Fact**
We can get great exercise.

**Fact**
It's a great chance to learn to use a compass.

**Fact**
We can learn about different kinds of plants.

**Fact**
There is only one show.

**Fact**
There is only one exhibit open right now.

**Fact**
We wouldn't be able to see the laser spectacular.

# Prewriting
## Organize

Use what I know to make a network tree.

your own writing

**Now it's time for you to practice this strategy.** Use the notes you took on page 111 to make your own network tree about your opinion.

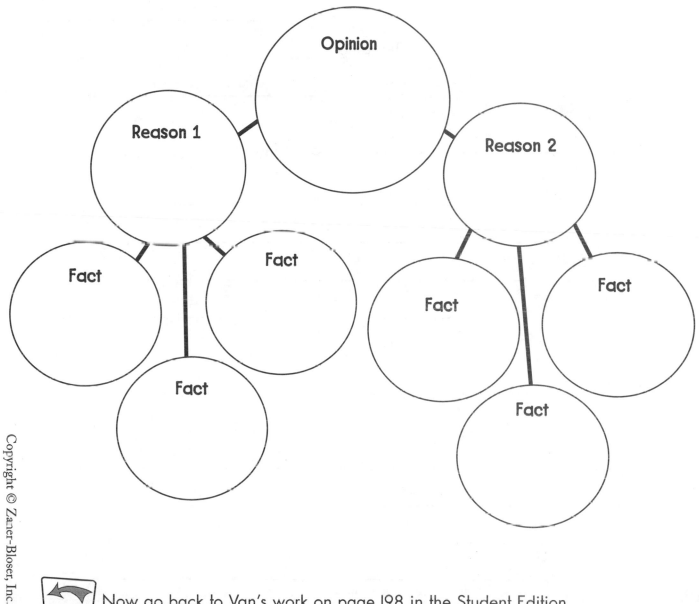

Opinion

Reason 1

Reason 2

Fact

Fact

Fact

Fact

Fact

Fact

RETURN Now go back to Van's work on page 198 in the Student Edition.

# Drafting

## Write

Draft my letter. Include an introduction, at least two reasons for my opinion, and a conclusion.

your own writing

**Now it's time for you to practice this strategy.** Use the space on this page and the next page to draft a friendly letter to persuade your reader about your opinion.

Heading _____

_____

_____

_____ Greeting

Introduction: _____

_____

_____

_____

Reason 1: _____

_____

_____

_____

_____

_____

**Persuasive Writing** • Friendly Letter

# Drafting

## Write

Draft my letter. Include an
introduction, at least two reasons
for my opinion, and a conclusion.

Reason 2: _____

_____

_____

_____

_____

Conclusion: _____

_____

_____

_____

_____

_____

Closing _____

Signature _____

Now go back to Van's work on page 200 in the Student Edition.

# Revising

## Elaborate
Add facts to support my opinion.

**Now it's time for you to practice this strategy.** Here is a part of one writer's friendly letter to persuade his teacher to take the class to Tracey Mountain on their field trip. After reading this paragraph, the writer noticed that he didn't have enough facts to support his opinion. Read the facts below. Write them in the paragraph where you think they belong. You will see some errors. You may fix them now or wait until later.

- We would be outdoors.

- We would get fresh air and good exercise.

- We are sure to see ferns, wildflowers, mosses, and mushrooms.

A hike would be fun and good for us, too! It would be fun

because we could move around. We could have a great time with

our friends We could talk and laff on the trails and in the woods.

On a hike, we can learn about different kinds of trees and plants.

We can learn about rocks and streems.

Remember: Use this strategy in **your own writing**

 Now go back to Van's work on page 201 in the Student Edition.

**Persuasive Writing** • Friendly Letter

# ReVising

## Clarify

Add signal words to show how my ideas are connected.

**Now it's time for you to practice this strategy.** Read this part of the friendly letter about the planetarium. Add signal words from the word bank wherever you think they are needed.

### Word Bank

| therefore | also | as a result |
| in addition | however | so |

The planetarium is not as exciting as it sounds. Some students might expect to see a laser show. That is not the case! The laser show is scheduled for Friday and Saturday nights only. During the day, when we would be going, there is only the show about the night sky. The planetarium is new. Only one exhibit is open at this time. We won't have enough to see and do there. We would have to stay inside and be quiet.

Remember
Use this strategy in **your own writing**

Now go back to Van's work on page 202 in the Student Edition.

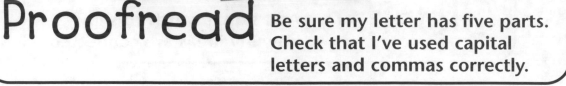

# Editing

## Proofread
Be sure my letter has five parts.
Check that I've used capital
letters and commas correctly.

⅃ Indent.

≡ Make a capital.

／ Make a small letter.

∧ Add something.

ℓ Take out something.

⊙ Add a period.

⧣ New paragraph

SP Spelling error

**Now it's time for you to practice this strategy.** Here is a revised draft of the friendly letter about the class trip. Use the proofreading marks to correct the errors. Use a dictionary to help with spelling.

14 South St.

Springer, Oh 98765

december 2 20___

Dear Mr. Swain

Everyone in our class is looking forward to the class trip in May.
Some students want to go for a hike on Tracey Mountain. others want
to visit the Powell Planetarium. I believe we should go on the hike.

A hike would be fun and good for us, too! It would be fun
because we could move around. We could have a great time with
our friends We could talk and laff on the trails and in the woods.
We would be outdoors. We would get fresh air and good exercise.
On a hike, we can learn about different kinds of trees and plants.
We are sure to see ferns, wildflowers, mosses, and mushrooms
on tracey mountain. We can learn about rocks and streems. We
will probably find tracks and other signs of aminal life. we can
observe birds. If some students don't know how to use a compass,
a hike is a perfect time to learn. As a result of all these things, a
hike would be a great learning experience!

**Persuasive Writing** • Friendly Letter

| Indent. | | Take out something. |
| Make a capital. | | Add a period. |
| Make a small letter. | | New paragraph |
| Add something. | | Spelling error |

**Proofread** Be sure my letter has five parts. Check that I've used capital letters and commas correctly.

The planetarium is not as exciting as it sounds. Some students might expect to see a laser show. However, That is not the case! The laser show is scheduled for Friday and Saturday nights only. During the day, when we would be going, there is only the show about the night sky. Also, The planetarium is new. As a result, Only one exhibit is open at this time. Therefore, We won't have enough to see and do there. In addition, We would have to stay inside and be quiet. Students would not have a good tyme.

I believe that going on a hike is the right choyce for our class trip. If you want happy, healthy students, please take us to Tracey Mountain.

your Student

*Brian McCaslin*

Remember: Use this strategy in **your own writing**

 Now go back to Van's work on page 204 in the Student Edition.

# Using a Rubric

Use this rubric to evaluate Van's friendly letter on page 205 in your Student Edition. You may work with a partner.

## Audience

Does the writer use language that is right for the audience?

## Organization

Does the writer state an opinion in the introduction of the letter, support it in the body, and restate it in the conclusion?

## Elaboration

Does every sentence in the letter add support to the writer's opinion?

## Clarification

Does the writer use signal words to connect ideas?

## Conventions & Skills

Are all five parts of the friendly letter included and written correctly?

### your own writing

Save this rubric. Use it to check your own writing.

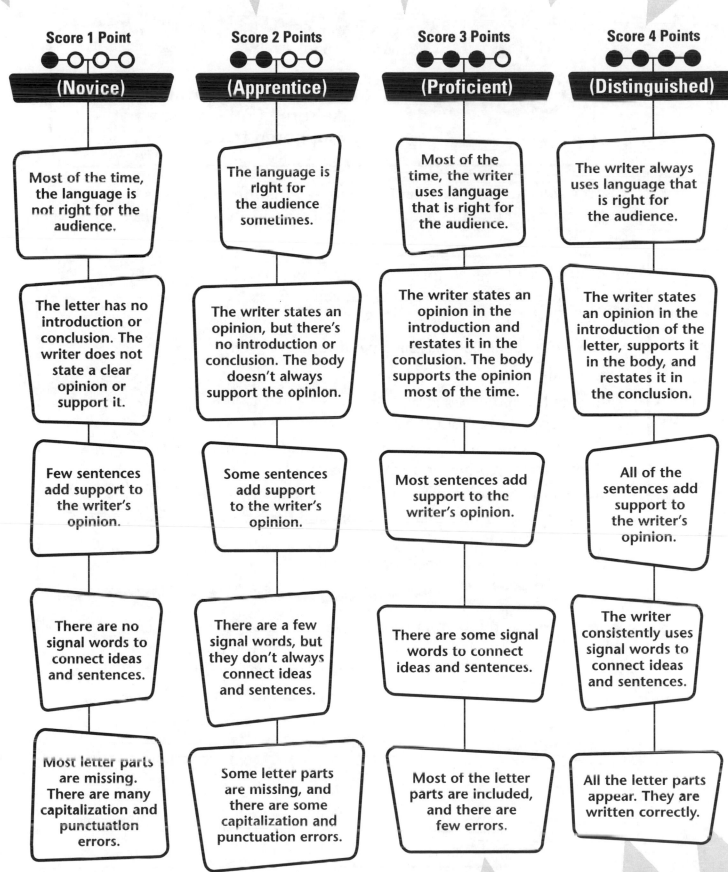

**Score 1 Point**
● ○ ○ ○
**(Novice)**

Most of the time, the language is not right for the audience.

The letter has no introduction or conclusion. The writer does not state a clear opinion or support it.

Few sentences add support to the writer's opinion.

There are no signal words to connect ideas and sentences.

Most letter parts are missing. There are many capitalization and punctuation errors.

**Score 2 Points**
● ● ○ ○
**(Apprentice)**

The language is right for the audience sometimes.

The writer states an opinion, but there's no introduction or conclusion. The body doesn't always support the opinion.

Some sentences add support to the writer's opinion.

There are a few signal words, but they don't always connect ideas and sentences.

Some letter parts are missing, and there are some capitalization and punctuation errors.

**Score 3 Points**
● ● ● ○
**(Proficient)**

Most of the time, the writer uses language that is right for the audience.

The writer states an opinion in the introduction and restates it in the conclusion. The body supports the opinion most of the time.

Most sentences add support to the writer's opinion.

There are some signal words to connect ideas and sentences.

Most of the letter parts are included, and there are few errors.

**Score 4 Points**
● ● ● ●
**(Distinguished)**

The writer always uses language that is right for the audience.

The writer states an opinion in the introduction of the letter, supports it in the body, and restates it in the conclusion.

All of the sentences add support to the writer's opinion.

The writer consistently uses signal words to connect ideas and sentences.

All the letter parts appear. They are written correctly.

# Prewriting

## Gather

Study the writing prompt. Make sure I understand what I'm supposed to do.

**Now it's your turn to practice this strategy with different topics.** Read the writing prompt below carefully. Think about what it asks you to do.

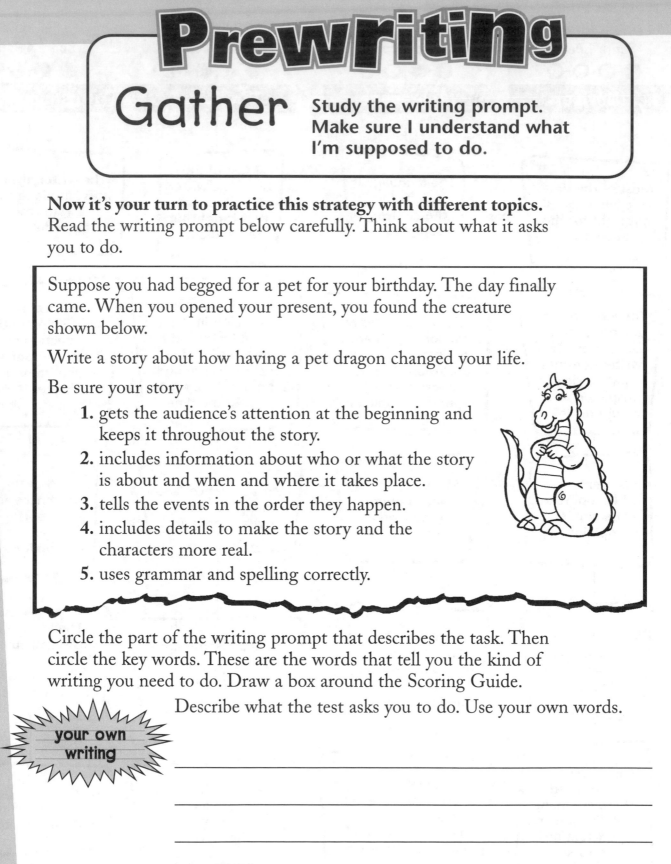

Suppose you had begged for a pet for your birthday. The day finally came. When you opened your present, you found the creature shown below.

Write a story about how having a pet dragon changed your life.

Be sure your story

1. gets the audience's attention at the beginning and keeps it throughout the story.
2. includes information about who or what the story is about and when and where it takes place.
3. tells the events in the order they happen.
4. includes details to make the story and the characters more real.
5. uses grammar and spelling correctly.

Circle the part of the writing prompt that describes the task. Then circle the key words. These are the words that tell you the kind of writing you need to do. Draw a box around the Scoring Guide.

Describe what the test asks you to do. Use your own words.

**your own writing**

_____

_____

_____

_____

RETURN Now go back to Joe's work on page 218 in the Student Edition.

# Prewriting
# Gather and Organize

Choose a graphic organizer. Use it to organize my story.
Check my graphic organizer against the Scoring Guide.

**your own writing**

**Now it's time for you to practice these strategies.** Go back and reread the writing prompt on page 122. Then fill in the story map to plan the story.

| | | |
|---|---|---|
| **Setting:** | When? Where? | ○ |
| **Characters:** | | ○ |
| **Problem:** | | ○ |
| **Plot/Events:** | | ○ |
| **Ending:** | | |

Some parts of the story map have a circle in them. These parts match up to parts of the Scoring Guide. Some parts don't match the Scoring Guide. Some parts match the Scoring Guide more than once. Write the numbers from the Scoring Guide that match the parts of the story map in these circles.

 Now go back to Joe's work on page 222 in the Student Edition.

Write

Use the information in my story map to write a story with a good beginning, middle, and end.

**Now it's time for you to practice this strategy.** Look back at the story map you made to plan your story about what happened when you got a baby dragon. Draft your story on these pages using your story map to write a good beginning, middle, and end.

# Drafting

## Write

Use the information in my story map to write a story with a good beginning, middle, and end.

_____

_____

_____

_____

_____

_____

_____

_____

_____

_____

_____

_____

_____

_____

_____

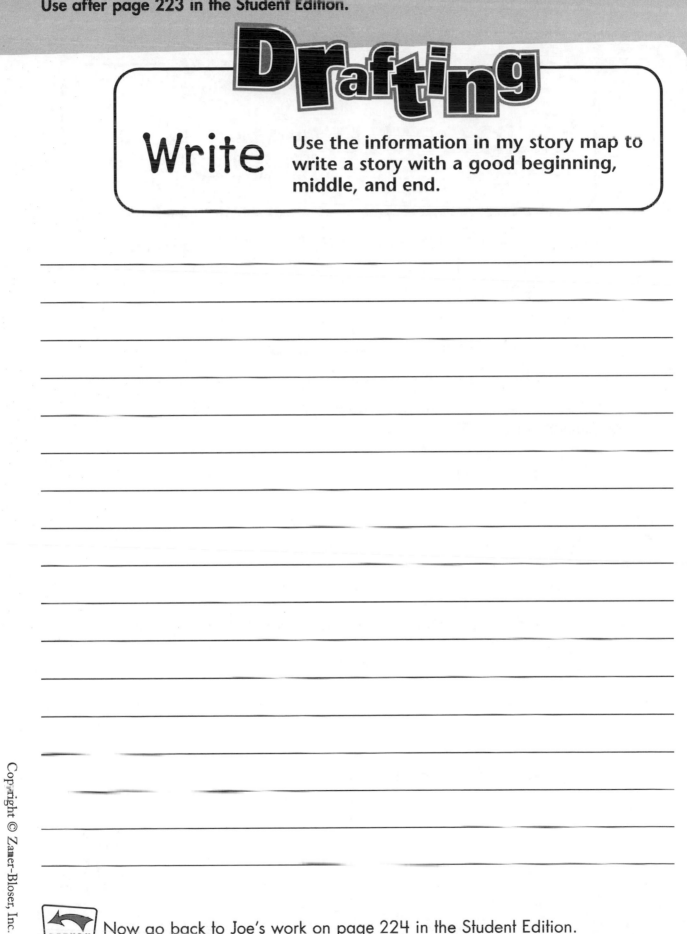

RETURN Now go back to Joe's work on page 224 in the Student Edition.

# ReVising

## Elaborate

Check what I have written against the Scoring Guide. Add what's missing.

**Now it's time for you to practice this strategy.** The writer of the following passage decided to include more details to make the story and the baby dragon more real.

Write the details below in the draft where you think they belong.

- For example, the dragon was always hungry.
- The whole neighborhood saved him scraps from dinner.
- The silly dragon whined when he saw anyone with an ice cream cone.

I was so excited to finally have my own pet. Little did I

know how much trouble one tiny dragon could make. That

dragon caused problems the minute I let it out of its cage.

Of course, little dragons grow up to be big dragons and

they need lots of food to get their.

Remember:
Use this strategy in
**your own writing**

Now go back to Joe's work on page 225 in the Student Edition.

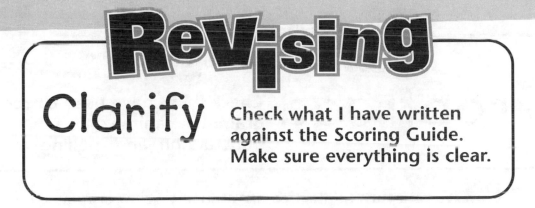

# ReVising

## Clarify

Check what I have written against the Scoring Guide. Make sure everything is clear.

**Now it's time for you to practice this strategy.** Here is part of one student's story. The writer realized that there wasn't any information about who or what the story is about or when and where it takes place.

Below are the details that are missing from the story. Write them where you think the writer should add the missing information. You will see some mistakes. You may correct them now or wait until later.

- the little baby dragon
- in May
- on my birthday
- We live in a small house.

I had begged for a pet for so long that I finally gave up

My mom always said we didn't have room for a pet. Then I opened

a present that would change my life. it wasn't the pet I had hoped

for, but it sure made things interesting!

Remember: Use this strategy in your own writing

RETURN Now go back to Joe's work on page 226 in the Student Edition.

# Editing

## Proofread

Check that I have used correct grammar, capitalization, punctuation, and spelling.

⌐ Indent.
≡ Make a capital.
/ Make a small letter.
∧ Add something.

℮ Take out something.
⊙ Add a period.
# New paragraph
SP Spelling error

**Now it's your turn to practice this strategy.** Below is a revised story about the pet dragon. Use proofreading marks to correct any errors in grammar, capitalization, punctuation, and spelling.

### The Ups and Downs of Owning a Dragon

I had begged for a pet for so long that I finally gave up We live in a small house. My mom always said we didn't have room for a pet. Then on my birthday in May, I opened a present that would change my life. it wasn't the pet I had hoped for, but the little baby dragon sure made things interesting!

I was so excited to finally have my own pet. Little did I know how much trouble one tiny dragon could make. That dragon caused problems the minute I let it out of its cage. For example, the dragon was always hungry. Of course, little dragons grow up to be big dragons  and they need lots of food to get their. The whole neighborhood saved him scraps from dinner. The silly dragon whined when he saw anyone with an ice cream cone.

Indent.

Make a capital.

Make a small letter.

Add something.

Take out something.

Add a period.

New paragraph

Spelling error

# Editing

## Proofread

Check that I have used correct grammar, capitalization, punctuation, and spelling.

Sparky caused more trouble that I have room to write about. as you know, dragons breathe fire. At first I thought this was a good thing, since my feet are usually cold. Then one morning I discovered smoke all over the ceeling of my room, and the sheets and blankets on my bed were all burnt. The final straw was the science project I had worked on for weeks. that dragon got a little too close and my project went up in smoke.

There are some good things about having a dragon for a pet the dragon and I had plenty of new visitors and friends. Sparky also scared away some bullys who wanted to take my lunch money. so I guess Sparky hasn't been all bad for my life.

**Remember:**
Use this strategy in **your own writing**

RETURN Now go back to page 229 in the Student Edition.

# Using a Rubric

This rubric for narrative writing was made from the Scoring Guide on page 209 in the Student Edition.

## Audience

Does the writer get the audience's attention at the beginning and keep it throughout the story?

## Organization

Does the writer organize the story so that events follow one another?

## Elaboration

Does the writer include details that make the story and the characters more real?

## Clarification

Does the writer include information about who or what the story is about and when and where the story takes place?

## Conventions & Skills

Does the writer use grammar and spelling correctly?

### your own writing

Save this rubric. Use it to check your own writing.

## Score 1 Point
### (Novice)

The writer doesn't get the audience's attention.

Events in the story are out of order. The story is confusing.

There are almost no details to make the story and the characters more real.

There is very little information about who or what the story is about and when and where it takes place.

There are many errors with grammar and spelling.

## Score 2 Points
### (Apprentice)

The writer gets the audience's attention at the beginning but doesn't hold it throughout the story.

Some events in the story are told in order.

There are a few details that make the story and the characters seem more real.

There is some information about who or what the story is about and when and where it takes place.

There are some errors with grammar and spelling.

## Score 3 Points
### (Proficient)

The writer gets the audience's attention at the beginning and keeps it for most of the story.

Most of the events in the story follow one another.

The writer includes enough details to make the story and the characters seem real most of the time.

The writer includes information about who or what the story is about and when and where it takes place.

There are only a few errors with grammar and spelling.

## Score 4 Points
### (Distinguished)

The writer gets the audience's attention right away and keeps it throughout the story.

All events in the story follow one another.

The writer includes many interesting details that make the story and the characters seem real.

The writer includes a lot of interesting information about who or what the story is about and when and where it takes place.

There are no errors with grammar and spelling.